WILD WEDDINGS

TRUE STORIES BY

Justice Dan Brookshire

SECOND
GUESS
PRESS

WILD WEDDINGS

First edition May 2020

ISBN 9780578232089

Design   SMoss

visit **www.justicedan.com**

to order **wildweddingsbook.com**

www.secondguesspress.com

SECOND
GUESS
PRESS

CONTENTS

WILD
WEDDINGS

Stacy & Miki

Happy Day

Dan

"If you want to sacrifice the admiration of many men for the criticism of one, go ahead and get married."

- Katharine Hepburn, actress

"Now I'm sleeping 'til the crack of noon, midnight howlin' at the moon. Going out when I want to and comin' home when I please. Don't have to ask permission, wanna go fishin, never have to ask for the key."

- Tom Waits, singer
from "Better off Without a Wife"

"I dreamed of a wedding of elaborate elegance, a church filled with family and friends. I asked him what kind of wedding he wished for. He said one that would make me his wife."

- Unknown

Dedication

To my wife Nancy
for all the magnificent things she has done

January 1980 our wedding ceremony
at Abbey San Encino in Los Angeles

Acknowledgements

I wrote acknowledgements for this collection a few years ago. I looked at it today and it is so stupid. I thanked childhood friends, relatives, movies, songs. Definitely stupid. I thanked everyone under the sun. Stupid. I am editing it.

I would like to thank everyone under the sun.

Thanks. All is One.

I would especially like to thank Heather, Derek, Hamilton, Evan and Connor for being my children, and Roxy for being my dog.

I would also like to thank Paula and Stanley for their hard work in this effort and appreciating my weirdness.

Dan
Norwalk, Connecticut
2020

Some sort of a Disclaimer

These are by far not the only ceremonies that I have performed over the years. Most were wonderful events. I have had many where there were 750 guests in attendance. One wedding had 1000. The majority have been between 2 and 150 folks. Most were elegant and friendly. Nothing about the better part of these ceremonies made them special, yet I am sure that the happy couples see it differently. There is little reason to write about those. When you have attended as many ceremonies as I have, most fall under the heading of boring.

However, the wedding ceremonies contained in these pages are off the wall, weird, unusual or just plain sick. As best as I can remember these are all true stories. Some have been easy to recall, while others were just a little purple-hazey.

This volume spans more than 20 years of marrying couples. As I try to record everything two decades later, some days I find that I don't remember why I sat down at the computer.

As you read these stories you may say to yourself, "this guy is full of it," and that would often be true. But this really is how some people got married. You couldn't make this stuff up. Truth being stranger than fiction, I have changed the names to protect the stupid.

It takes all kinds

Couples come in all shapes, sizes, colors and varying degrees of weirdness. They can be financially disabled or average middle class. Some are rich and some are extremely rich. A disproportionate number of the extremely rich are not kindly people. All couples do fall into three categories:

1) Together, cool and ready to go.
2) Clueless as a bag of hammers
3) The Totally Disengaged

Together, cool and ready to go are my favorites. They call, they pay right away, we put it together, then I do my job. Simple, over and out.

I less prefer the Clueless. They take forever to confirm. They have 10 legitimate questions and thousands more stupid ones. It is very exhausting dealing with their friends, their mothers, their aunts and their selves. With them I'm often obliged to hang around and make small talk with the groom. Always, always, there is one friend or relative who knows everything there is to know about weddings and how exactly the day should go. I must remain very sweet and tolerant with these fools. At times I have been forced to be less than likeable to get my point across to a know-it-all maid-of-honor or bridesmaid. I had one bridesmaid give the finger to the back of the head of the one that was giving me a hard time. That was hilarious and immediately softened my approach to her.

Even less do I like the Totally Disengaged. It is always the same. Grooms that don't give a hoot about the wedding. Brides that control their future husbands by the ring in their noses. Most of the time, rich or poor, they have neither manners nor social skills or are just plain low-lifes. Dirt mongers and money grubbers. They could be anything from tow truck drivers to Wall Street wolves. When they first contact me, I can tell if they are going to just waste my time. If their first question is "How much?" I know that they are going to shop around and go with the cheapest. Many say, "Oh great, I am so glad that I found you, it sounds perfect. I will go to your site and pay today." Three days later, still nothing. I usually follow up with an e-mail. Of course I get no reply.

A Justice of the Peace can't hold grudges or harbor ill feelings. Common courtesy, a return call or an email make a difference. It's not that difficult. Just email and say, "Sorry, we found someone cheaper, better and you're ugly." The Justice of the Peace doesn't really care. Just let a guy know!

The origins of the Justice of the Peace

The role of The Justice of the Peace originated in England in 1195. King Richard I commissioned certain knights to maintain peace in disruptive areas. These knights were responsible for ensuring that law was upheld. They answered only to the King. They were known as "Keepers of the Peace." That title changed under the reign of King Edward III in 1361. The King instructed that "good and lawful men" be appointed to each county to guard the King's peace. These men were called "Justice of the Peace." Until the establishment of county councils in the 19th century, JP's fixed wages, had roads built, controlled all commuter routes and bridges, provided and supervised all services which Parliament and The Crown deemed necessary for the welfare of the country.

Today I say a few magic words, and poof! married. I scope out the women, eat an unfair share of shrimp and get paid more than an entire village population in 1195 ever made in their entire miserable medieval lives.

In America as early as the 1600's, JPs were commissioned to handle minor civil and criminal cases. In the 17th and 18th centuries, and on behalf of the English Crown, the primary duty of the Justice of the Peace, among other roles, was the administering of local government. In my state of Connecticut the position of Justice of the Peace has a history dating back as far as 1686.

While the authority of JPs has diminished over the years, a Connecticut JP today is authorized to give oaths, take depositions, affidavits, acknowledgments, serve summonses, and of course perform marriages.

In the 21st century, the state of Connecticut determines the number of Justices in each town. The positions for each city or town are allocated to ensure that the two major political parties are equally represented. Each party selects JPs from candidates officially registered with the party, one-third by the Democrats, one-third by the Republicans. The remaining third are selected by non-affiliated candidates. You must be affiliated with a political party, be in good standing in the community and can only be appointed in a Presidential election year (every four years).

Rather than be detected, inspected, selected, elected and possibly rejected by either party, I found the way around. I switched from Democrat to Independent then selected and elected myself, bam!!!

WILD
WEDDINGS

I was sorry I said that

Just before performing a wedding in an old historic restaurant in the next town, I put my foot in my mouth big-time. I had spoken to the groom on the phone a few times and he was cool. We had a quick guy-connection, so that is why I thought I could speak freely.

The restaurant had two areas. This wedding was in the small room to the right. As people arrive, me and the groom stood in the foyer. Wedding guests "to the right please," all others coming to the restaurant for brunch "to the left please." After a few minutes of this, in walked a guy I recognized. I didn't know him personally, but I had seen him enough around at local events and at my kid's school. I knew the guy to be loud, always going, very high-energy. Within a half mile this of guy you knew it was him. He came in the door talking loud to the people with him. He was in street clothes and I didn't notice the garment bag over his shoulder. Without thinking I leaned over to the groom and said, "I hate this guy." So of course the groom leaned into me and said, "that's my brother."

A bunch of Wall Street chumps

One of the first ceremonies that I ever did was at a country club in Greenwich, CT. Nice place, not great. There was lots of golf activity going on all around. Lots of mothers in white tennis shorts dropping off their kids so they could go home and have private tennis lessons with their young instructors.

Through this whole wedding ordeal I didn't meet anyone of particular merit. The bride was a big doormat and did whatever her Wall Street jerk of a fiancée told her to do. The groom was condescending, rude and brushed me off. All his groomsmen and all her bridesmaids were rude to me. I had to confer with them to get the procession and recession routines straight. But they were not having any of it. They would not listen to my recommendations. It was their friend's wedding. They should respect that. I gave up. We marched out on the deck, I performed something resembling a ceremony. They were all talking and fooling around during the entire proceedings.

The kicker is that the groom had only paid half my fee in advance. After the ceremony I asked about the balance. He hemmed and hawed and wandered in and out for about half an hour. I was ready to go home. None of his relatives or rich bigshot friends had any cash to chip in. Finally I left. Never heard from them again. Truly a man who always got his way.

A family affair

I was to do a wedding in a small town upstate. A few weeks before the ceremony my wife and I take the drive to the place where the wedding was to be held. To get to this place we travel 8,000 miles to nowheresville, turn left off a rural road onto a side street that makes a horseshoe and empties back on the same road. The town consists of a historic hotel (George Washington slept there) a house next door and two abandoned one-story industrial type buildings across the street. The wedding is supposed to take place across the river from the abandoned electrical plant. We drive over a small one-way bridge to check the place out. There is absolutely no parking, so I park precariously on the side of the road with almost no room, uphill on a curve. I walk into the woods and find the overlook. The drop over the edge is precarious. Only a very small ancient one-foot high wood rail will hold people from falling to their death. The rail may have been built by a bear. It is odd, old and very unsafe. The gigantic electrical plant looms on the other side of the river. No one is in sight. It looks like a 1955 monster movie scene where the monster meets its end.

The wedding day arrives, and I am back at the one-way bridge. On the other side I see an old red pickup truck revving for first rights to crossing. I am writing this years later and though I don't remember who won, I think one of us died.

Again, I park in a dangerous spot. Eight guests arrive. Where did they park? Most guests are in jeans and flannel shirts, including two girls holding hands. The groom's men wear brown tuxedos with puffy Paul Revere and the Raiders shirts. The bridesmaids each wear what look like their prom dresses. It is a happy affair. A two-year-old boy gets lost. Everyone panics – did he wander off and die on the curve in the street, in the woods or over the edge. He is found not too far away sitting on a rock, holding a dead squirrel.

A gazelle as payment

A few days ago, I put an ad out to barter my Justice of the Peace services.

Almost immediately I received a reply. A guy in upstate Connecticut offered me a gazelle in trade for performing his daughter's wedding ceremony. As I was a little more than curious, I e-mailed him right back. "A gazelle?" I asked, "Do you mean like lion food?" He replied, "Well, yes in a way, but I would hope not."

My son Hamilton said, "Yeah, let's get it."

My wife Nancy said that we don't need a gazelle.

I'm thinking we do!

A very particular bride and it all goes wrong

This bride was very precise and very particular in every way. She had everything planned out to a tee. She insisted that I come to her home for lunch to discuss every aspect of the day. Most of which did not involve or concern me. I think that she wanted to flex her control over everyone involved, and she did. As usual, I listened, expressed interest and then I just went with the flow.

The wedding was held at a hotel spa on the Sound about an hour from my home. The sky threatened rain. The venue rep said that we would move into one of the ballrooms if it rained. It rained. But not before 100 of us were all in place on the beach. When the deluge started we all ran for the hotel, which was about 50 yards away. After a few minutes the bride made the decision to go back outside and try again. We did. Just as I started to speak the rain started again, hard. Lots of screaming, laughing and running. The bride had about 10 handlers. Inside again we went.

The staff set up a ballroom with chairs and small candles along the aisle. I started the ceremony by saying, "you know what they say about rain on your wedding day." I heard about 10 people say, "it's good luck!"

The couple wanted to read a little something to each other. The groom had written a short sweet paragraph. Bridezilla's little something was five pages long. In our consultation she had wanted me to read it. I told her it would be more meaningful coming directly from her. In a humorous way I told the guests that her speech was so great in length that when I finished reading it, I fell in love with the guy myself! After her 10-minute monologue, I began to read a small piece about love but I couldn't finish it. I started to cough. I couldn't stop, it was persistent. A busboy came down the side and handed me a glass of water. Thank you, young man. I started again.

About three sentences into it, out of the corner of my eye I noticed flickering near a lady in an aisle seat. Nothing out of the ordinary about that, except that the candle on the floor had ignited her dress and she was about to be enveloped in flames. Pointing, I said, "Excuse me miss, but you're on fire!" Three or four people behind her were already on the way to her rescue.

Fire and rain. What a memorable day for this bride who had meticulously planned her wedding for 33 years.

The valet brought my car around as the sky turned beautiful and clear.

A walk in the park

After a ceremony *on an early Saturday morning in New York City, I decided to take a walk-through Central Park. I sat on a bench near the Bethesda Fountain for an hour, then took a slow walk toward the subway station, stopping occasionally. This is what I heard on that day.*

****

As I was sitting on a bench, two little girls ran up and sat down. Sisters I would guess. One was about 7 years old, the other about 5. As their mom and dad passed, pushing a stroller, Dad said, "Ashley, Taylor, come on girls let's go." Without batting an eyelash the older girl says to her little sister, "Ignore him."

****

"I wonder how Yoko is doing these days?"
"Ah, who gives a damn?"
Two elderly women sitting near Strawberry Fields.

****

"It was huge and coming right at my face, and I thought, YUMMY!"
A 20-something guy talking to a woman he was walking with.

****

"And I thought it was a giant bear until he shut the door and stepped into the light."
One girl to another.

****

"Comment pourrait-il 150 années?" (How can he be 150 years old?) An old French woman to another.

****

"Are you kidding? She can't wear white!"
A woman talking on the phone.

****

Kid #1: "Tom and Jerry are not real, you moron, they're cartoons!"
Kid #2: "No, they're not. I saw them on a show."
Kid #1: "They are ink, you idiot, they're ink!"
Brothers.

****

I saw a well-worn woman in her 50's crying while talking on her cell phone. On the bench next to her lay a giant pile of used tissues. She was speaking in a dialect so foreign that I couldn't even begin to guess what it was. It sounded a little Arabic, maybe part Italian and somewhat like the bleating of a goat. She finished her conversation, wiped her eyes, gathered up the evidence of her sorrow, stood up, smiled and walked away.

****

"And how would *you* set the table, mother?" A woman walking very fast and talking to herself, obviously long-traumatized.

****

A young couple and her parents walked by. The father-in-law says, "Robert, point of interest, what building is that?" Clearly

Robert had answered a thousand point of interest questions today. Miffed, and not hiding it, Robert turned and said, "What now?" The father-in-law points and Robert says, "That's the Gulf & Western Building." As they walk away with her parents in front, Robert's wife, their innocent little daughter, put her head on his shoulder reached around and squeezed his manhood. He smiled and put his arm around her.

****

Michael Jackson died a few days ago and there were no less than 15 impersonators in the park. None were any good. Tourists were paying $5.00 to have a picture taken with them.

A wedding in colonial New England

I once married a young couple in a 350-year-old historic church in Newtown, CT. This beautiful white building stands at the top of a hill on a roundabout. In the middle of the traffic circle is a flagpole with an American flag. The immediate neighborhood is grand. Great stately homes line the street, Victorians, Mansard, Colonial and Colonial Revival. This church dates to the early 1600's. At some point in time it was moved from the original location to where it sits today. Inside it has high back pews and a wraparound balcony. I imagine that many a three-pointed hat sat in those very seats. They had kids that stayed out late. They had a mortgage, and horses they had to take care of for transportation, food to grow and Indians to watch out for.

I said the vows standing on the third step leading up to the stage area. The bride and groom stood on the floor in front of me. Another semi-low cut bride's dress. From my perch three feet above I could see the bosoms completely. I am a professional, but still, this is always distracting. I am sure that every guest said to someone else, "did you see her breasts?"

After the ceremony everyone, except the bridal party, went outside. I was standing next to the bride as she was arguing with her new hubby about where to take pictures. At that moment I noticed a good-sized spider crawling up the side of her dress.

For a moment I wondered if I should wait to knock it off. I watched the spider climb. I stepped forward and brushed at it when it reached waist high. She didn't acknowledge me touching her at all. She didn't even stop talking.

They decided to take pictures later at the reception. Then they turned and walked out the front door. The guests blew bubbles as the newlyweds got into a car and pulled away. Within one minute everyone else scattered and I was left standing on the steps by myself. I heard the heavy church doors shut behind me. Sixty seconds ago there were lots of people, confusion, laughing, yelling, and moving about. Then in a matter of seconds I was alone. Not a parting word was said to me by anyone.

This wedding may not seem like a significant story, but for me it's a rather unique experience. To have the opportunity to preside over a marriage in a 350-year-old colonial church in New England was something very special. History embraced me and that was what made it worthwhile and memorable.

All American, strange American

I don't remember in which New York village or county this wedding took place. I know it was around 85 miles up the Hudson River from New York City and about one hours' time from my house in Connecticut. I don't remember much about the couple. What I do remember however, is that they and everyone at the wedding were just perfect, perfectly strange.

To get to the groom's parent's house where the ceremony was held, I had to drive on one of the most scenic roads ever. The small tree lined, two lane, country road curved along the side of green pastured hills overlooking valleys of horse farms, silos, barns, beautiful country homes and pastures. White fences ran for miles. It reminded me of the Lake District in England, without the lakes.

I drove up the winding road to the house. I saw a deck with many people mingling about having a good time. I got out of my car and a rather too excited man approached me with his hand extended and said, "Hi, I'm Bob." I replied, "Hi Bob," but before I could get my name out, Bob already had his arm around my shoulder and was walking me to the house. "You're Dan, the Minister," he said. His excitement was a little tingly. Bob walked me up onto the deck and announced, "This is Dan, our Minister." Everyone yeas. I looked at these delightful folks and I noticed that this was a J Crew ad. Someone had opened a giant catalog above us, and J Crew mannequins fell out all over the deck. An all-American crowd. There were beautiful knits, sweaters tied over shoulders, lots of Khaki, no socks. I could see $140 haircuts on all the men.

Even stranger than this was everyone seemed beyond happy. I got not just a smile from everyone I was introduced to, but a huge over the top smile, hello, and handshake. I also noticed that even when someone was getting a drink or standing by themselves, they had a huge smile on their face. Everyone was very happy, happy, happy. I avoided the punch. When I went upstairs to speak to the bride, I found a boy about 5 years old in the hallway playing with a real sword. It was a bit heavy for him, but he was trying. The railing was open to the living room below. To avoid any bloodshed I took the sword away from him. He was not happy.

Outside they had set up kind of a campground area with logs to sit on, and a flowered arch for us to stand under. At the appointed time we all waited in place. However, the bride still had not come out.

Ten minutes later she strolled down the aisle wearing a lavender and lace long dress trimmed in fresh flowers. She looked hippie beautiful. During the ceremony two bees would not leave her alone. In spite of that we pushed on and got through it. Her perfume had probably attracted those bees. It attracted me too. She smelled wonderful.

I was far from home and it was late afternoon. I stayed for dinner. Great barbecue.

Finally I said my goodbyes to everyone and walked to my car. About four or five of the happy campers walked with me. This was weird. As I pulled away, I looked back and I saw them running after my car and their smiles were grotesquely gigantic and they bared pointed sharp teeth that were slobbering blood and saliva. I sped off. That's what I hate about upstate New York. All the damn vampires.

And in a backroom voice she said Lola

I was at a wedding in a very refined waterfront home here in town. It was about 20 minutes before game time and I was standing in the living room checking out the backyard. There were lots of pretty people milling about, laughing, hugging, drinking. As I stepped out onto the deck, I noticed a rather tall woman leaning against the seawall, sipping out of a large empty glass. I thought: this woman is not what she seems. I can see all the telltale signs. She was tall with broad shoulders, muscular arms and legs, huge feet. I wandered around, and noticed that no one talked to this woman, she stood alone.

I take my place under the pergola ready to begin the ceremony. During my reading I can see the mystery woman sitting on the end of a row still sipping her nonexistent drink, eyes on nothing particular. The ceremony is over, and everyone gathers to congratulate the newly married couple. The mystery woman stays on the outskirts then regains her place on the seawall, not saying a word to anyone. In time I asked the bride who this seemingly shy woman is. "That's Bobby, my cousin." She tells me that she thinks that this is Bobby's first time out as a female. She asks me if it bothers me. I tell her of course not and that I hope she doesn't feel awkward. I say that I am going to talk to him. The bride corrects me, as in talk to "her." I stroll over and introduce myself. She says, rudely, "I know who you are." I ask her name, she says, "My name is Lola." I try hard to make conversation, but Lola isn't having any of it. She may feel misunderstood and like an outcast, but I'm trying to be inclusive and make her feel comfortable. I ask her if she lives here in town. She shoots back, "Nope." She never looks at me. I tell her that her cousin is a very lovely girl and makes a beautiful bride. She chuckles at this like a smartass.

I say, "Nice talking to you, Bobby," and I walk away.

And so does her vagina

A friendly couple called and wanted to get married at Fairfield Beach, about 3 or 4 miles from my home. I am to go to their house and then we will do a short walk to the sand. The bride-to-be is a free spirit. She is European and is dressed like a hippie. The wedding party consists of the bride and groom and a young girl about 7 or 8. I don't recall whose child she was, the bride's or the groom's. Their good friends came in from New York and brought their daughter also about 7 or 8 years old. The spot where they wanted to say their vows was about 40 feet wide and about 30 feet from the water. It was rocky with no sand, just mussel, oyster and clam shells, on the water with a great view. It's all about love and that is what counts. The kids ran around and threw things. The sun was setting.

In many cases I am asked to snap a picture or two as it was this time. I was handed the camera. I posed the bride and her friend sitting next to each other on a rock. The little girls on each side and the men standing behind. I looked through the view finder and made sure they were smiling and posed well. OK, there's the groom and his friend. I look down, OK, the little girls look good. I glance at the girlfriend and she looks fine. The bride looks delightful. So does her vagina! I can see her vagina. Complete and intact and smiling back. She is sitting on the rock with legs akimbo and no underwear. What should I do? I squashed my first instinct to drop the camera and run. But then they would say "What the heck was up with that guy"? Or they'd develop the film and get a surprise. Or perhaps simply take the picture and then, as I hand the camera back, ask for a copy?

Naturally I did the right thing. I told them that the sun was too bright, and I asked them all to move about a foot to the right. Click. Six people and no vaginas.

Another mob wedding

Down along Long Island shore in New York, there are many old country clubs on an outlet called Davenport Neck in the town of New Rochelle. The Siwanoy Indians had been hunting and fishing and thriving in this area on Long Island Sound for thousands of years. Then the white man showed up in the 1600's. A white settler from Westchester, N.Y. petitioned the Governor for a claim on this rather large portion of shoreline. The claim was given, then revoked. The settler waited for the next governor - his buddy - and the claim was then granted. The state told the Siwanoy Indians to get lost.

The old mansions were built anywhere from the mid 1800's to the 1920's. I have performed dozens of wedding ceremonies at these grand old homes that dot the coastline. Most of these places were turned into country clubs in the early part of the 20th century. Up until the late 1960's these local social clubs were probably cookin! Swimming, eating, drinking, sexing and lots of partying.

I have been to this club many times. As I open the giant door it's like the "Wizard of Oz" except it goes from color to black and white. I observe a sea of mid-length black leather jackets on the men. All of them sport the same 50's Elvis style hairdo, not a single hair out of place. I think all these guys are made men. Picture them with Elvis hair and Joe Pesci's face. Most of the women are in fur and while many are attractive, many looked like middle-aged worn out adult movie stars. Most all the woman wear lots of makeup and it appears hard for them to stay balanced in heels made for younger feet. It may be the booze. I am sure that these women have a lot to drink about to make the world look new again.

The groom is in his 30's, while the bride was well north of 40. She is sloppy pretty. He is short.

Things are running late, so I stand in the foyer gazing. As I look out among a field of black hair, I see a shifty eyed guy looking around. He is wearing a leather mid-length jacket and a black turtleneck. I peg him for the hit man. I smell crazy on him. I am absolutely sure that he has a gun, and I am absolutely sure that he is not the only one present packing heat.

On the other side of the room I can see the elders. Short happy gentlemen with drinks, cigars and big pinky rings. There's not a woman in any of these circles. Not allowed. Next to the cloakroom I see two bald guys who must be the accountants. They are in three-piece suits and are not wearing black mid-length leather jackets. These accountants are in a heavy conversation with three guys wearing black mid-length leather jackets. The conversation doesn't seem to be going well. One of the Vinnies softly grabs accountant #1 by the back of the neck and shakes him lightly and smiles. I see accountant #2 start to take a step backward but in an instant, he realizes that would be a wrong move. Vinny lets go and with the other Vinnies he walks away. He turns back, using his finger like a gun points to them and smiles. To me, everyone in this building is a suspected murderer.

I made conversation with a few people before I left. "Where are you from?" "How do you know the couple, are you a friend of the bride or the groom?" I think to myself, "You idiot, you weren't paying attention! *I am* the Officiant!" I was having a talk with one guy in a black mid-length leather coat and eventually I asked him where he was from. He stopped, looked at me seriously, asked why I wanted to know.

As I was leaving, I saw the couple and the photographer walking toward the beach to take pictures. The bride was wearing a black mid-length leather jacket.

In the parking lot, a car backfired, and everyone hit the ground.

Are we being followed, or what?

It was 2:00 in the afternoon, a Friday, and I was home alone. I was nodding off on the couch listening to "Dear Mr. Fantasy" when the phone rang. I picked it up and before I could say hello, a strange voice spoke, "Are you the Justice of the Peace?" He sounded like Peter Lorre, the scary actor from the 1940's. With some hesitation in my voice said "Yes I am."

The voice asks if I can marry someone real quick. I ask when they are planning to get married? He says that they want to do it today at my house. I pause and then tell him that I can do that and let me tell you how to get here, and what time would you like to come? "We are in front of your house now," he says.

I look out of the window and I see a grey four door sedan parked at the curb. I can see a man behind the wheel and a young couple sitting in the back. The guy tells me to come out. Without waiting for a response he hangs up. I get dressed and go outside. As I approach, the front passenger window goes down. "Get in" the driver says. It's the voice from the phone call again. I bend down and look in, checking these people out. The couple in the backseat are in their 20's. They seem normal enough. The woman says," It's OK." How many times has she said this to some poor, innocent shmuck who they've kidnapped and locked in their basement until the ransom has been paid? With some reservations, I got in.

The driver looks dead. It is 90 degrees out and he is wearing black leather gloves. I scan the car for weapons. I ask if they have their marriage license. With eyes staring straight ahead the driver pulls a white envelope out of his vest pocket and hands it to me.

The groom asks if this can be done while we drive. I tell him I guess it's OK, as long as we stay in the city limits. The car abruptly takes off and I am pushed back in the seat. I look at the driver. He is constantly checking me out with sidelong glances. Sometimes he is speeding and then he turns a corner and goes excessively slow. It hits me, they won't kill me because I have to sign and file the marriage license.

I didn't expect to be doing a ceremony driving around in a car, so I didn't prepare vows. I winged it. As I am talking to the couple, each one takes turns looking out the back window. Just before they say, "I do," they both look out the back window. Is there someone or something after us? Her dad? The cops? The Mob? Frankenstein?

But really, I don't want to know, and I am too afraid to ask. I want to go home. Like waking from a dream, we pull up in front of my house. I get out, turn, and as the car speeds away I say to nobody in particular, "I'll file this Monday morning."

Halfway up the walk it hits me. I didn't get paid.

At the fantasy beach

Weddings on the beach can be very cool. I did one at a home right on the water about 45 minutes up the coast. The couple were in their late 30's or early 40's. They seemed like good people. They had both been married before and had two children each, 8-year-old boys and 12-year-old daughters. The boys were off doing something most of the time. Both girls were named Heather. They stuck together like glue. Pretty, young model types, they spent most of the day giggling.

A tent had been pitched on the sand right in front of the house, about 50 feet from the water. It being the weekend, there were lots of other people on the beach. Kids were running around screaming and playing, yelling for sandwiches and kicking balls.

I didn't stay and socialize this time, although I wished that I could. At the time, my wife was home nursing an injured foot and wearing a robo-boot. Somebody needed to go food shopping. I said that I would go on my way home after the ceremony. I was hungry too. My wife's last words to me were, "Hurry back!"

I was hungry. After the ceremony I walked toward the house, headed for my car. I entered the backyard, stopped dead in my tracks. In front of me were two young women in their twenties, wearing crisp white bibbed aprons and tall chef's hats. They were sitting on either side of a big black cooker full of lobsters. To my right I saw a pyramid of corn-on-the-cob. To my left they were dishing out fresh steamers! One of the nymphs says to me, "Are you joining us?" My stomach is screaming "Yes, yes, oh yes!" But I couldn't get the vision of my hungry family at home out of my head.

Soon, I was rolling around in the sand eating steamers while these two chefs wearing nothing but butter- soaked aprons fed me lobster. At least that's what I was fantasizing about minutes later as I was driving home hungry, on my way to pick up peanut butter and toilet paper.

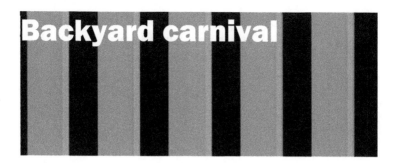

Backyard carnival

After cremating my dear Mother-in-Law, I flew home on the redeye from San Francisco. The wedding had been booked for months, so I could not back out. I was cutting it very close. The ceremony was scheduled for 3:00 P.M. and it was on the Connecticut / Mass border. It is a long drive from the airport. Just a few days prior a bridge on the 95-turnpike caught fire and melted. I-95 was a parking lot. There were so many detours that I was an hour late to the wedding. But for the same reason, most of the guests were late an hour or more. They just partied until I got there. Later that day people were still arriving as I was leaving.

The place was about 3 acres and easily 50 kids under the age of 10 were running everywhere. The slip-n-slide was in full use. The Beach Boys music played loudly. The bar was a piece of plywood standing on six milk crates. Two blenders continually whirled up margaritas. An uncle acted as the bartender. He sported a grass skirt, coconut shells over his chest and a teeny-tiny red cowboy hat. I was the only one in a suit and it was about 90 degrees.

For the ceremony they set up rows of rented chairs. I stood under the awning. I wanted to start by apologizing for being late. But before I could say a word an 800 year-old woman holding a red party cup shouts out, "You're late." I start to explain but she starts to grumble. A voice from the back yells, "Be quiet, grandma." Grandma comes back with, "Oh, f*#k you." The guy, who is standing in the back, says, "No, f*#k you, grandma," and laughs. The DJ kid is ready to hit the music. He is looking at me waiting for my cue. I point with force, the kid hits it and five seconds of Lynyrd Skynyrd blasts out. About 5 seconds later it stops, and Whitney Houston begins to warble.

I finish, and the couple seems happy. Walking to my car on the hill above I look back down on this menagerie, shake my head and count my blessings.

Bad song people

I did a wedding ceremony at a forgettable wedding venue. Wedding venues can be pretty cheesy. Fake Roman columns, grand staircases. I had been at this place before.

I first met the couple at my home for a consultation. They were a cool, hip couple in their late 30's. The groom was a happy go lucky kind of guy, always smiling. The bride-to-be was very agreeable and asks me what I would like to eat, the chicken or the fish. The groom adds, "You are staying for dinner right?" The bride chimes in, "Please, we would love to have you." I'm liking these people so I tell them, "We'll see."

The big day arrives and the ceremony goes fine. Before dinner I find myself sitting at a table. The bride and groom, holding hands, pull up right on me. "You said you're staying for dinner, please say you are!" I'd just given them a humorous, well-received wedding ceremony. I have to say yes.

Just as I said that, the song that I hate the most in the world blasts out of the speakers. The bride screams throws her hands up and yells, "I love this song!" and spins off singing and dancing. The groom smiles at me, waves and dances away.

It was the first of a horrific music marathon. Each and every song that DJ played, I despised. These people managed to find every song that I have ever hated in my whole life. The bride danced madly on the dance floor. A parade of nightmare hits.

When I met them they seemed so cool. Yet every song got progressively worse. At one point I thought about checking to see if my ears were bleeding.

I said my goodbyes to the couple and fled. Outside, I bashed my head against a tree about 20 times. Then I drove away.

Caucasian debris wedding

In politically correct terms, this wedding was total Caucasian debris.

I met the couple at my home a few months prior. In talking to them for only a few minutes, I knew that the wedding was going to be nothing but a big backyard party. I quite like this kind of ceremony, but usually I am the only one in a suit.

The location of the wedding was at a lost in the woods pig farm in rural Connecticut. Vintage trucks without wheels decorated the landscape, accented with bizarre rusting farming equipment of unknown purpose. Covered tents with plywood on the grass served as dance floors. The Marshall Tucker Band was blaring out of a boombox, while from another boombox not far away, Sweet Baby James blasted. There was a lot of farm fashion present. Everyone was related in one way or another. Like at a small-town carnival, many activities were set up and in full use. This was to keep the 20 kids occupied.

I went into the house to see the bride. There were aunts and moms all cooking up a storm in the kitchen. I found Crystal, the bride, in the upstairs bedroom getting ready, all her girls crowded around. Farm fashion at its best. We talked, she handed me the marriage license and I told her how pretty she looked. I said nothing about her ridiculous headdress. I asked where I could find her husband to be, Tracy. She didn't know. One of the girls said, "I saw him with Shelly in the barn."

Crystal stopped cold. "Really." "She is lying, Crystal," another helpful girl piped in. "Amber, you're a b-i-t-c-h. Why would you say that?" Amber said, "God, you guys, I'm just joking. They were behind the barn." Crystal laughs, "F-you, Amber." Amber is tailgate pretty and trashy hot.

Crystal's mother pops her head in. Crystal asks her if she knows where Tracy is. She says that he is behind the barn with Matt. Everyone laughs. Mom explains that they are getting saw-horses to make another table. Mom says, "What, did you think they were back there blowin' each other?" That was one of the funniest things that I had ever heard come out of a mom.

I wandered down the hill and around the back. I saw a bar set up in the basement and went in. The bartender was straight out of a western movie. Down at the end of the bar I spot trouble. This guy looks like Matthew McConaughey in "Dazed and Confused." He has a comb over and is wearing a three-piece suit of a khaki-ish color like you might find in a baby's diaper. The knot in his tie is almost down to his belly and a corner of his shirt hangs out. He is sweating profusely. He may have just snorted all the cocaine in the Western Hemisphere. Leaning on his elbow he looks up at me and says, "Who are you, the preacher?" I say that I am the Officiant. He yells at me, "Well, if you're good enough for Crystal and Tracy you're good enough for me!" and slaps the bar really hard. It must have hurt. He yells at me again, "I'm Gale, and what is your name, man-at-the-bar with me?" "I am known as Asclepius," I answer. "Say what? Is that even a word? What kind of name is - is whatever you said?" I remain silent. He says nothing then begins to yell, not sing, a KC & The Sunshine Band song. He's already had too large a helping of loudmouth soup. I tell the bartender that he probably should not serve this guy anymore liquor. The bartender tells me that Gale came in like that and after the second insult he has been giving him seltzer with booze just on the rim. We pump fists. Not his first rodeo.

Still, everything went well. Everybody happy. As I was driving out, I saw one of the bridesmaids between two cars making out with a girl with tattoos and big boots.

Note: *Asclepius, a demi-god hero in ancient Greek mythology. It is also the nickname that I gave myself as a teen.*

Chumps in the parking lot

What I do remember is the rehearsal.

The day before the ceremony we all met at the venue for the rehearsal. We had to use the parking lot due to an event inside. The bridal party was larger than usual, seven on each side. Everyone was in the bar when I arrived. Once we got them out to the parking lot the bridesmaids were very cooperative. But the groomsmen were skunk drunk, loud, obnoxious, laughing, wandering off, generally unruly. They kept their beers in their hands.

I felt like a lion tamer. I had to get these freaks together to rehearse for tomorrow's ceremony. Nobody cooperated. Eventually I was forced to call in the big gun.

I walked over to the bride, who was in conversation with the venue rep. I asked her if she could help me with this, I pointed to the groomsmen standing around, being stupid. A look of shock came over her face, then anger. She went over and turned the air blue. She was swearing, yelling, pointing and pushing. I thought that she was going to slap a few of them. That brought them down, but they were still wise guys.

The ceremony definitely happened the next day, yet all I remember is that angry bride yelling at a bunch of drunken wise guys in the parking lot. Only she could have set them straight!

Disturbin' in so many ways

A young woman called from Arizona to set up a date for her wedding to be held at her parent's farm in upstate Connecticut, right in the middle of nowheresville.

The directions seemed sketchy with way too many turns over the hill and far away. This was before GPS, so of course I got lost. The country roads had few street signs. But in the bride's description of the turn into her drive she had mentioned a 'blowed up' mailbox. I rounded a curve and there it was. I turned in. The drive went uphill about 100 yards and at the top, I saw two men standing dead center, both wearing top hats, matching vintage suits with tails. One man was about 6'5" and turned out to be the groom. The other, his best man, stood no more than 4' tall. They both had beards. It was a strange illusion, the two wearing identical period piece suits. From that moment forward I thought of them as Lincoln and Lil' Lincoln. I got out of the car and introduced myself. I noticed piles of discarded objects everywhere, lots of rusted metal and appliances.

After the requisite small talk with the Lincolns, I went into the house to meet the bride. The ranch style house had been built into the rocks. The bride's father was sitting in his chair wearing a blue and white flannel shirt and a pair of jeans. He had a Pabst Blue Ribbon beer in his hand.

I met the bride, her mother and a few of her friends. After a few minutes of small talk I asked for directions to the restroom. The mother and daughter looked at each other and giggled. Mom said, "through that door." I opened the door and it was like the grotto at the Playboy mansion, not as elaborate, but made out of stone and big. It was both cool and creepy.

Outside, Lincoln and Lil' Lincoln were standing in the exact same spot as where I had left them. 15 or so guests stood about saying nothing. Two cowgirls appeared from around the back of a big metal shed. They were the real thing, jeans, vests, hats and boots. I learned later that they were both in the Air Force stationed in Arizona, a couple, partnered. There was an old car with four flats. Nearby I saw an old bus raised up on blocks. Later the two cowgirls told me that they were "bunkin" in there.

It must have been 90-degrees that day, so I decided that it was time to get this sideshow on the road. "Let's go," says I, with much authority and I head up the trail through a forest of refrigerators and car doors. Everyone follows me. Like a huntin' dog, Lil' Lincoln darts ahead. Big Lincoln is taking long strides just like the long dead President would have done. The piles of metal and junk open up to a wagon rutted road. Suddenly I realize that this is a Christmas tree farm. These people can't be all that bad. They love Christmas!

We round a bend where a white tent canopy occupies a wide spot in the road. To the left is a mosquito infested pond in a lovely shade of green. To the right there is a grove of Christmas trees. Under the awning there is a table with a CD player probably broadcasting "Dueling Banjos." On the table there is an arrangement of 25 small hotel-size liquor bottles. We all stood around on a huge rectangle of 2' x 2' carpet samples of various colors and textures. We waited and waited and waited and then waited some more. I was making small talk with Lil' Lincoln and it got hotter. Finally from down the road a guy in overalls yelled, "She's ready!" A minute later, from amongst the

Christmas trees, an engine roared and black smoke shot up into the air. It really startled me. "What is this?" I said, but not under my breath. Lil' Lincoln looked up to me. "What did you say?" I ignored him. I look over at Big Lincoln and he is picking his nose. I return my attention to the smoke and noise. Over the tops of the Christmas trees, the bucket of a backhoe rises into the sky. It was the purdiest backhoe I ever did see. The bucket was all done up real fancy like, with purple ribbons, white bows and everything!

And in that backhoe bucket sat our beautiful bride. Dad, Pabst Blue Ribbon in hand, was driving. The bucket came closer and closer and ever so gently lowered the bride on to the row of 2 x 2s which led up to her future husband, a path to eternal bliss. I see that Big Lincoln has a wide smile on his face and is sweatin'. His bride looked much the same. They both cried.

Love is a wonderful thing. I congratulated friends and family. Big Lincoln was downing a small bottle of champagne. The bride was looking for an Allman Brothers CD. A few feet away near the malarial pond Lil' Lincoln held a mini bottle of Ol' Crow in one hand and was trying to catch a grasshopper with the other. Dad was standing on the road holding his hat, staring up at the sun.

I swapped a few roadkill recipes, said farewell to all and headed for civilization. On the way out I saw Lil' Lincoln kneeling at the pond, Lil' liquor bottle in hand. I yelled goodbye. He stood up turned toward me real fast and waved. He was chewin' on something.

Fall from grace

I did a wedding for a South American guy and his beautiful fiancée. She was from Poland or Russia, and very pretty. They obviously had a big language barrier and could barely communicate. I suspected that she was marrying him just to get citizenship. Around 30 friends and family came for the ceremony, some all the way from South America. They were clearly his relatives, all Spanish-speakers. Out of misguided respect these nice people were addressing me as "Your Honor" and "Judge." One man called me "Supreme Judge." I told him that a simple "Sire" would do.

The bride knew *nada* Spanish. She was still upstairs when I arrived and was to make her appearance when the music began. The CD started and at the top of the stairs she readied herself for the first step. We couldn't see her because the stairs were blocked by a wall. She took the first step and fell head over heels, tumbling down in a mass of white, like a snowball rolling down a hill. She hit the bottom, boom! The Latin aunts, mothers, grandmothers, sisters and nieces all screamed at once, as if Julio Iglesias had walked in. They all ran to help her. A few of them knocked heads as they swooped in. One minute all was well, the next thing I knew I was staring at a mass of screaming curvaceous Latin American backsides. She stood up, looking for a face to connect with. She probably wanted her mommy. She locked eyes with me, I held out my hand and said to her "You're OK?" and she smiled and said yes. I held her hand and walked her to the spot to take their vows. The groom was nowhere in sight.

I had the chance to talk to her afterwards. I remember she told me she didn't know this guy for very long. She was very evasive about the rest. I wondered how this couple got together. When a bride is alone and has no family throughout the whole marriage process, it can be sad. In the past young women have asked me questions that they should have asked their mom or dad.

I stayed for the toast, said my goodbyes and walked out to my car. The newly married couple was standing on the porch. She looked at me, raised her hand slowly, stopping waist high and gently waved. It was poignant, leaving her there like that. It reminded me of dropping off my kid at camp or college and looking back at them in the rearview mirror and seeing them fade in the distance.

First gay day

The day that Connecticut legalized same-sex marriages happened to fall on a Saturday. City offices are normally closed. Andy Garfunkel, the town clerk at the time, was very progressive on the matter. He opened the clerk's office on that day with balloons, cookies and other festive stuff. He was right in his thinking that many couples wanted to get married on the first day that it was legal. Andy let the Justices know that the office would be open, and to stand by. I lowered my normal fee to a gay discount for the occasion. Word spread.

My first appointment happened to be my sister-in-law's cousin and his partner. I did a few more marriages that same day. One guy whose ceremony I performed bounced his check, but I never chased him down. It was enough to be a part of such an auspicious moment.

I believe that I married the first same-sex couple in the State of Connecticut.

Five guys in tuxedos and a girl from the Bronx

A heavy accented man living in New York called and wanted to set a date to get married in my home.

On the day of the ceremony, a car pulled up in front of my house. A skinny guy got out of the car followed by four more skinny guys, clearly from another country all wearing tuxedos, all talking at once in some dialect that was just plain wild. Getting out of the car behind them I see the bride. She was wearing a business suit that looked like it came from JC Penney. She looked shell-shocked. The guys paid no attention to her. They came up the walk and into the house jabbering all the way. The woman was lagging way behind. The men stopped in the foyer frantically fumbling with a video camera. They were loud with skinny arms flying about.

The woman skirted this and went into the dining room, sat and said nothing. She looked bewildered, sad and scared. At this point I sensed something is rotten. I am thinking that this is an arrangement. This guy needs a green card. A JP friend of mine got wise to this scam. He had couples that were looking for legalization that were being filtered through a Kentucky Fried Chicken in Times Square. I guess the guy making mashed potatoes ran the immigration department at KFC as well. He would match them up and then send the couples up to Connecticut to get married. When my friend figured this out, he cut it off.

As they fight for the camera, I take the opportunity to talk to the bride. I ask if she is feeling alright and if she would like a glass of water. She says "yes, thank you." I ask if she knows this guy. She says that she does. I ask if she wants to get married today. She says that she does. I can tell that both answers are a lie. I then tell her that she doesn't have to do this and that I will give her a ride home. She says that it is OK and that she wants to do it. I stall for a few minutes while these guys try to figure out the camera. I want to give her more time to think about what I said.

But she married the guy, giving us a new American citizen. Not 30 seconds after the "I do" the guys ran out the door, leaving her behind. She looked at me and shyly said goodbye. I told her to make sure to call a friend if she needed anything. The groom came back for her. The guys waved and yelled, "Thank you, Mr. Dan."

Just a few weeks ago the groom was pulling a goat cart, and most likely is now driving an illegal cab in Queens.

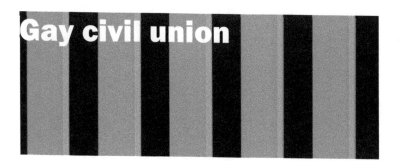

Gay civil union

Before same-sex marriages were legal, couples had to settle for a civil union. This meant that couples had some rights as married couples, *some rights*, but not the same rights.

A couple of guys in their late forties set up a ceremony to be held at their friend's home in New York. It was an impressive, beautiful, big home along the Hudson River. This was an affluent affair – you could tell by the well-dressed kids running around. A few days before the ceremony the guys called and asked me to read something about the history of bias against gay people over the centuries.

So I scribbled a group of what I hoped were cool words. When I read it, it got some people thinking and a few laughing. I said that in days past it had been legal for convicted felons to marry while in prison, but not these two fine gentlemen who obviously love each other. I had a lot of folks say kind words after my reading. The buffet was bountiful, I stayed late.

It had been raining lightly all day. Three valet guys were taking cover in the garage. I asked for my car and experienced my own tiny moment of discrimination. One of the valets said, "Sure, which car is it?" I said, "A black Mercedes." He said, "Yeah, right, everyone wants a Mercedes, what kind of car do you have?" I point and say, "That black Mercedes right there." The rain picks up. I could have just walked to my car, a quick sprint across the driveway, but now that valet deserved to get wet.

Hammonasset again

On a hot Friday I had a rehearsal up the coast on Hammonasset Beach, a long way from home. I have done a few ceremonies there in the past. It's quite a drive, up past New Haven and beyond. I encountered big time traffic on that Friday at 5:00pm.

Hammonasset Beach State Park is Connecticut's longest public beach, 2 miles long. Hammonasset means "we dig holes in the ground" and was named by the native Woodland Indian farmers who lived along the river until you-know-who showed up. The first colonists arrived in 1639. The native Indian's land that they had farmed and lived on for 10,000 years suddenly got smaller and continued to shrink until the natives had a just little corner way over there. And now it's parking, and very expensive parking at that.

Through the whole planning stages of this wedding I only dealt with the nutty mother. No doubt she was a direct descendent of those colonists. She held back $100 of my fee to make sure that I would show up. Perfectly understandable. It was also understood that she would pay for my parking for the two days. The rehearsal proceeded. I met the happy couple and the bride was gentle and oddly attractive. The groom looked a little punch drunk, and reminded me of Joe Walsh of the Eagles.

The day of the wedding Nutty Mom called me twice when I was within 10 miles of arriving. I am not there more than 5 minutes and they start getting out food and begin to have lunch. I actually joked that I didn't drive an hour and 20 minutes and brave traffic to watch them eat. Between bites some of them laughed. They did have shrimp, so I availed myself of that.

I married the couple, the band played, and everyone had a great time. I was there an extra 45 minutes because I first had to watch them eat.

The mother paid me the $100 but then said that she would not pay me the $30 for two days of parking. I stared at her for a few seconds and then said, "Really?" She answered, "Really." I told her that was not our agreement and she just looked at me, but didn't say a word. I said, "OK, thank you." I sought out the new husband and wife and said goodbye and good luck. On the way out, on behalf of the Woodland Indians, I helped myself to a salad bowl, filled it with $30 worth of shrimp and grabbed a bottle of water out of the ice bucket for the ride home.

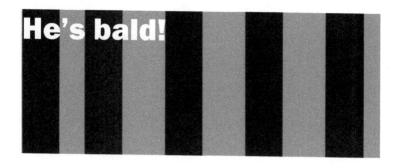

He's bald!

There is a concert every year in Bridgeport, CT called, "The Gathering of the Vibes." It is a four-day concert, sleepover, with festivities, food and booths that sell candles, incense, tee-shirts and weird things made out of wood. It is an annual celebration of The Grateful Dead.

I was called by one of the promoters to perform a wedding ceremony for him and his girlfriend during the concert. I happily agreed. I think the headliners that year were Phil Lesh and The Black Crows. I wore white casual attire and a white Panama hat. The concert attracts around 15,000 each year. I do remember that there was only one guy that was not wearing a tie-dyed shirt ... me. I grew up in Southern California in the 1960's and to this day I have never, ever worn a tie-dyed tee shirt, not my thing at all. However I have taken LSD and stared at them for hours.

Before the ceremony I hung around the VIP tent. I walked around gathering good vibes. People came from all over the country for this celebration of the Dead. I had a pass around my neck so folks didn't think that it was strange that I would randomly walk into their campsite. I talked to people I didn't know from my old neighborhood in California and I met people that came from The Netherlands. It was a throwback to the concerts of my past. It is very strange to see a 17 year old or a 20 year old hippie chick with long hair with a small ring of flowers in her hair and in her hand, wearing a long tapestry or a tie-dyed dress with a halter top, smelling of patchouli oil. I remember the pioneers of this look. These weekend hippies cannot be in the same place as our girls of the sixties. However, the present now will later be past.

The couple that I am to marry are very flower power-ish. They want to do their vows near the water. They choose a spot and we begin. Of course there are thousands of people all around us. Clowns on giant stilts, jugglers, idiot drunks, high happy people and just your run of the mill concert freaks. A crowd of 500 or so gathered to watch the ceremony. At one point during the ceremony my hat blows off. A drunk wearing a tie-dyed Hawaiian shirt and holding a beer, yells out, "He's bald!" Some near him laughed but I think that they were laughing at him due to his drunken stupor. Out of the crowd some guy yells, "Yeah and you're drunk and ugly." Everyone laughs, including me. A girl pops up and puts my hat on my head. She turns toward the crowd and with clenched fists she raises her arms in victory, people cheer.

As I ate up a fruit bowl, I hung out and watched some bands. When I got to my car and there was a punk cop sitting on it. I said, "Hey man." With a mean-cop look he just walked off. He had to move the barricades so I could get through. Good vibes.

High rise in Brooklyn

I was sitting in my office at home on a Friday at 3:00pm when the phone rang. "Hi Reverend Brookshire (some people call me that) are you almost here?" She was calling from Brooklyn, on a holiday. It was a rare occasion when I messed up and forgot. The ceremony was scheduled for 3:45. To make matters worse the ceremony was to be in her apartment in downtown Brooklyn 40 miles away.

This lady had changed the date, time and location twice. Nevertheless, I should have kept better track. I told her that I was already on the road but there was a lot of traffic and that I might be a few minutes late. She said that was OK, all the guests were not there yet. I put on most of my suit and flew out the door. As I got to the N.Y. line my GPS was directing me into Manhattan. I thought this can't be right. Normally I would be going over the Whitestone Bridge, through Queens and into Brooklyn. You should never argue with GPS, you will always lose. After heavy traffic on the turnpike, I am now in much worse traffic on the FDR headed downtown and it really sucks. Between just getting onto the FDR and the Brooklyn Bridge, 6 or 7 miles, the bride calls me no less than 4 times. I lie and tell her a bum was hit by a car on the FDR, and the traffic is backed up. I reach the Brooklyn Bridge at 3:45. If you have ever driven across the Brooklyn Bridge into Brooklyn you know that it is absolutely insane. Millions of people walking everywhere, millions of cars driving every which way and every street is under construction. I begin to worry about where I can park. It looks like nowhere. People in the city sit in their cars and wait for people to die so they can get the parking spot. A guy once said that if you are going into the city and you find a parking spot in Jersey, you park! I am driving through neighborhoods, bumper to bumper construction all the way.

Four o'clock and I arrive at her building. It is a new building and probably the tallest in Brooklyn. As I pull up a guy straight across the street vacates a spot. An amazing bit of luck.

The lobby is huge. As I approach the desk the doorman leans back, and with two fingers he points and says, "The wedding man!" I was only 15 minutes late and the bride was totally OK with that. Some guests were still arriving.

The apartment is on the 25th floor and has fantastic floor to ceiling windows with views of both Brooklyn and Manhattan. The apartment is very small and accommodates six comfortably. However, so far there are about 30 people packed in here. She wore a traditional African ceremonial costume. He was a little standoffish. A few relatives had yet to arrive, so we waited 20 more minutes before we began the ceremony. Still, I think the groom was put off because I was late. I could tell that his opinion of me was not good. I agreed to be there at 3:45. I wasn't, and I apologized.

I did the deed. The couple are happy, everyone is happy. I leave, but I am not so happy. I am about to get on the Brooklyn Queens Expressway at 5:00 P.M. on a Friday.

Hot Rachael

This is not about the couple, it's pretty much about Rachael.

This was a ceremony for a couple in their late 40's at their home across town. It was a traditional old place, built sometime between 1875 and 1900 I would guess. The road was a well-used thoroughfare back in the years before the Revolutionary War. I remember some school field trips at the river near there. George Washington traveled on this road going to New Haven and then on to Boston. If you look hard enough you can still find markers, which are stones sticking out of the ground just big enough to put an abbreviation for Boston and arrow pointing the way. There is one on the corner of my street.

The yard where the ceremony was to be held is enclosed with a proper white picket fence with trees and bushes that block the view of the street. There were tables with white linen and about 40 people in attendance. I met up with the very tall groom and after some small talk I asked him for the marriage license. He said that he had been looking for it earlier but couldn't find it. We went looking. On a window seat there were stacks of papers from one end to the other. This guy started digging in. I stood and watched. After a few minutes I drifted over to the kitchen. There were a lot of women doing cooking things. A caterer was there preparing as well. I love checking out old homes. I usually wander around. Knowing that I am "The Man" nobody ever questions me. I drift back into the dining room where the groom has been looking for the license. A few minutes more and he finds it. I saw him pull it out of the middle of a pile of envelopes, papers and junk.

We went out on the big old wide porch to find the best spot to do the nuptials. The bride came out and I was a little taken aback by her attire. Although it was kind of cool, it was a little bit scary too. She looked like a witch on Halloween, lots of orange, black and purple. We figured out the best spot, and they said that we can begin in about 20 minutes. The bride then introduced me to her daughter. Enter Rachael. Rachael was over 18 and under 25, and promiscuous for sure. She was thick, shapely and already drunk. She was wearing a short little summer dress and three sheets to the wind, perfect!

After all these years the chronological order of how things developed is hazy. Sometime later Rachael asked me if I wanted to see the house. Of course I said yes. When we got upstairs, we were in her parent's bedroom. The bed had 4 posts. Rachael grabbed a post and did a little stripper move. It was innocent. She just swung around holding the post. This ample breasted girl swinging on a pole in a low-cut summer dress looked good doing it. This could have been the beginning of an adult film. A four poster bed, a young pretty girl and an old fool.

We did the ceremony on the porch. These people were cool, so I stayed for food and drink afterwards. I met the bride's sister. This lady seemed way out of place. She was upper crust for sure. She was attractive, articulate, and intelligent. She worked for a large corporation in Washington D.C. I spoke to her for quite a while. To my right was a table with a Goth girl sitting alone. I moved next to her and we spoke for a bit. She was definitely alienated. Suddenly, Rachael appeared out of nowhere and plopped down in the chair next to me. She was still liquored up. Seconds later she spun off toward the house. Rachael's boy toy had now arrived at the table talking to the Goth girl. As it turns out he had just been in a serious motorcycle accident. He showed us the humongous scar on his chest. An Evel Knieval wanna-be. He said to nobody in particular, that he had to go home and change his shirt. He seemed in pain and slowly got up and walked out the gate and got on a Ninja bike and without looking, roared out into the street. Two guys came up to me and asked if I wanted to go out back and smoke some pot. Rachael came back into view, stumbling all over the place. Across the yard there was a stone bench. Rachael turned to sit on said bench and missed it completely. She landed on her butt in the dirt. People nearby reached out to help. They picked her up and lifted her over to the bench. I said, "don't light a match near her." She sat down and promptly rolled right over backwards and into the bush. Goodnight, Rachael.

I just drove away

Every once in a while, a couple will want a relative to perform their ceremony and just have me make it legal. That is always OK with me. I still have to suit up, show up and do the paperwork. This couple wants the groom's mother to read it. I email back and forth a few times helping with the wording and whatever tips I can offer to make things go as smoothly as possible.

This ceremony is at an old mansion turned wedding venue in New York, on top of a hill overlooking the Hudson River. It's a hot day. I estimate it to be about 4000 degrees outside.

I have an alternative plan. In the bridal suite I have the marriage license and I am going over the vows with the mother. I tell her that I can marry her son now and she, the mother, can do the whole ceremony without me. She likes that idea. A sister leaves to find the groom and is back in just a few minutes with him in tow. I ask the bride and groom if they wish to marry each other and they both say yes. I say, "I pronounce you husband and wife." The witnesses sign and that's it. The mother says that I can sit with the guests instead of up on the platform. I am not sitting in 4000-degree heat to watch a wedding of people I do not know.

I told the groom that I was going to put the marriage license in my car. Which I did, then quickly drove away.

I love dogs, just not these dogs

I did a ceremony at a small stone castle on a lake in New York. The view, the lake, and the castle were all perfectly picturesque.

The couple, Samuel and Helen, were in their late 40's and from Vermont. Samuel looks like the cowboy actor Sam Elliott. He is dressed in denim. She is pretty, a hippie chick wearing a yellow summer dress, a circle of flowers and ivy on her head, and she is barefoot. They are very cool people, earthy. They had a few goats, some chickens, a garden, cats and 5 retarded dogs. Other than the animal kingdom, no human guests, just we three.

I pull up to the house and right away the dogs are on me. Going crazy all around my car. I don't know what breed they are, but these are big dogs, hairless dirty dogs. One look and I could tell that these dogs are seriously undisciplined. I am concerned for my safety. When I get out, they will jump on me for sure. Helen appears and tells them to all settle down. Since they evidently don't understand English, they just keep going about a thousand miles an hour, in circles, bouncing off the car, each other, off Helen, just falling and slobbering all over the place. Dogs who don't listen. Sam shows up and with a little more authority orders the dogs back. They keep going nuts, just slower.

As I step out of my car, they all try to hump me at once. Sam and Helen both jump in and save me. Jokingly, I ask them which one is Cujo. They laugh for a few seconds and both point to the white dog, "That one." Helen tells me to stay clear because the dog hasn't eaten since yesterday. Sam says that he did eat today. She says, "No, he hasn't." Sam says, "Yes he did, remember, the mailman." Helen smiles and says, "Don't believe him. He tries to scare everyone with that stupid joke."

We go in the house and they let the dogs right in behind us. The mutts are running all over the place sliding on the wood floors crashing into walls. A grey dog sits next to me slobbering, then sprints off.

We do the ceremony in the living room. The dogs are running between us bumping into my legs. One dog starts barking loudly at the door. Sam lets him out. Two seconds later the crazy canine is barking to get back in. Before Sam can open the door more than two inches, the hound pushes his way back in and bounds around the room like he has never been inside a house before. The dogs are their family and they want their family present. If these were humans, they all would be wearing helmets.

Helen had a fruit plate set out and some bread that she had made. We were talking names and I mentioned that the name Helen was kind of old school. She said that actually her name is Katheryn but she took her grandmother's name. Of course she did, and she bakes bread too and lives in a castle on a lake with horny animals.

I tell them that they seem very happy together and what an unbelievably beautiful corner of the world they have. I ask in jest if they need a caretaker. Sam says that they get a new caretaker every year, but they always disappear. Helen says not to believe him and that he always tries to scare people with that joke. "Only two have gone missing," she says.

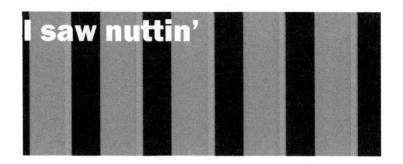

I saw nuttin'

I only remember 3 things about this wedding:

1) It was on Staten Island.
2) It was at night.
3) Maybe there was a murder.

After the ceremony the guests and myself were in the backyard. The party was in full force and man these people loved to drink. These were local citizens, pretty girls and big guys with unclear professions. There were more BMWs out front than a dealership. I was having a wine spritzer. Before I left I noticed a scrawny guy already drunk. He was slurring and loud. I don't think that he had a date. He didn't look like the others either, he looked like David Spade. I went to say goodbye to the bride and groom, we chit chat for a few minutes. Then I head out through the back gate. I see the drunk guy arguing with three big boys. The little guy is poking his finger into one big guy's chest. I stop to watch. They all start to move around him a bit. Suddenly two of the guys pick him up under the arms and the third guy opens the back gate that leads into the woods behind the garage. About two minutes later the big boys came back ... without the little guy. I quickly head for the driveway, I made no eye contact, I looked down until I got to my car and I said to myself, "What did I just see? I saw nuttin', I saw nuttin', I wasn't even there." I said this to myself repeatedly all the way home.

I was busted watching porn

A couple came over early one evening for a quick wedding. With them were the brother of the groom, his girlfriend and two other guys. They were all from New Jersey. They had their own vows written out. I mixed it with the usual verbiage that makes a ceremony. The bride cried, the groom cried, the brother cried. The other two guys did not. They took a few pictures. The groom tried to slip me a little something, but I politely refused. They were going out to dinner here in town. I told them that it was their night and to go enjoy themselves. Thanks all around and they left.

I went upstairs and changed clothes. Once back downstairs as I pass through the foyer, I notice an envelope with the couple's names on it. I call the bride and tell her about the envelope. She thanks me and says that they will come right back and pick it up. I put the envelope back on the table in the foyer and I go into my office to check my email. Twenty minutes go by and they still have not shown up. An hour went by, still nothing. I take care of some business, surf the net. I opened an email from my old friend Bob Jeffers, who lives in California. I usually open his mail with caution as it often contains something perverted. Sure enough it was a video of two attractive women in the heat of passion and one was very vocal in expressing her delight. After about 15 minutes of this I went out to the front door. I see that the envelope that was on the table is no longer there. The couple must have come in without me hearing them, retrieved the envelope and then simply left. I am sure that they peeked into the living room. From there the office light around the corner can be seen. So I surmise that they came in, heard a woman screaming "Oh yeah, right there, right there, right there!"

They must have heard this woman's voice coming from the back office and just slipped out without saying anything.

I would hate to have that as my wedding day memory. But then again, they have a great story to tell.

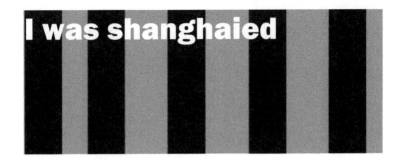

I was shanghaied

I did a wedding ceremony on a 175-foot yacht out of Stamford. It was a hot, hot humid day, 108 with the heat index. Of course I was wearing my black suit. We did the ceremony on the upper deck. It was so hot that the bride told me to skip all the jive and just say the important part. There were about 150 guests sitting in the boiling summer heat and humidity. When I came out, I addressed the crowd with, "I am going to do this in under five minutes." There were audible sighs of relief. From the rear of the seats I hear, "Yea!" I do it in four minutes. Afterwards, I make an announcement for everyone to go one deck down for cocktails. Once there almost every guest came to me and thanked me for the quickie.

I found the grandfather of the bride sitting alone at a table. I pulled up a chair next to him and introduced myself. He was in his 90's and came over from Ireland. About 15 minutes went by and I happened to look out of the window across the room ... we were moving! I shot up, turned around and opened the curtains behind us, we were moving! I started telling people around me that we were moving! A woman said, "Yeah, it's a boat and boats do that sometimes." I had not been told that this ship was going anywhere. It was going somewhere. It was starting a four-hour trip on Long Island Sound, six o'clock to midnight. I had not heard the engines rev up. The music was playing but I heard nothing. The ship was so big that you really don't feel movement. I went looking for the first mate. The captain can't turn around, he said. It would take an hour. They didn't call an "All ashore," because no one was going ashore.

I told him that I had meant to go ashore! I probably sounded like Gilligan. I saw the Connecticut shoreline drift by as we picked up speed.

So I wandered around for four hours. While everyone knew each other I didn't know a soul. They played a lot of Enya, which is just colored air.

The sun went down. I talked to a chain-smoking pretty girl on the upper deck. I talked to the staff. I talked to grandpa again until he nodded off. As the officiant I can most always go anywhere I want at a venue. No one has ever questioned me. They think that I am a Priest or Reverend or Bald Jesus. So in this case I went up to the wheelhouse, opened the door and asked permission to come in. The captain asks, "Are you the officiant?" I say, "I am." He says, "Ha, I hear that we shanghaied you, sorry about that." I say, "Yeah, well the same thing happened to me off the coast of Rangoon once." He gives me a puzzled look. "Really?" he says halfheartedly. I tell him that "I am not sure, but I think it was me." Now he looks at me like I am nuts, but he laughs. I hung out for a while, killing time. We got along well. He was a navigable guy.

When we returned to port and as we were docking, everyone headed aft. I make my way almost to the front of the crowd. People are yelling jokes about boats, and everyone is quite or somewhat drunk. As we stand there people are still saying thanks for the short ceremony. One guy says loudly "let's give the Reverend a hand." Yells, claps, whistles all around. I clasp my hands over my head and shake them. Next to me, a very inebriated semi-sexy, sloppy woman, 48ish, swaying in the warm breeze and still holding a drink, says, "Hey, let the Reverend through, let him up front." With her leg she pushes the guy in front of her aside.

I eventually did get off and returned to the thick, humid summer air. I got home at 12:10 A.M. It wasn't what I had planned for the evening, but I made the most of it. An unexpected moonlight cruise.

I was so hurt today at the reception

This could be by far the strangest wedding I ever performed. A woman in her twenties called and set a date for a quick ceremony at my home. She called a few days later and changed the time. She called the next day after that and changed the date. She called yet again to change the time and asked if she could bring friends. I told her that I could not make any more changes and yes, she can bring a few friends, limited to five.

On the day of the wedding she calls and says that she will be late. She shows up 45 minutes later than her late estimate. I am standing looking out of my living room window when I hear a car with no muffler coming up the street. It passes my house, stops and backs up stopping in front. Six people get out. They are a budget version of the Jersey Shore cast. Two goons were wearing cheap black blazers, and another was wearing a red corduroy jacket. They all had black shirts, no ties, big sunglasses, new white sneakers and lots of bling. Like in a cartoon, the car backs up a little bit then, bam, a big blast of smoke and off it roars. Some old lady, the three goons and the bride all flick their cigarettes into the street. There is also a girl maybe 10 years old with them. I didn't see her smoking but that doesn't mean that she wasn't. They all walk up to the door and I let them in, bringing with them the strong smell of cheap cologne. An elephant could have choked.

The bride is wearing a strapless white wedding gown that showcases her numerous homemade tattoos. She had more tattoos than teeth. I asked her for the marriage license and the fee. She says that she has the license but forgot the money. I tell her that she should go get it. She says that she will call her husband. She asks one of the goons for his cell phone. She dials and standing next to her, the younger goon's phone rings, he answers. She says, "Where are you?" He waves and says, "Right here!" She asks, "Why are you answering?" and hangs up. She dials another number, no answer. She can't get a hold of him. I'll work that out later, I thought. Right now I am focused on getting this done and getting them out of here. I hear the junk car pull up in front of the house. The groom has arrived.

The uncle asks me how much my house is worth and then asks how much the armoire cost. He says that he has some knowledge of antiques. Some of the guys slouch in the chairs. I hear a few "get outta heah" and a lot of "Yo." They think that they are so cool and all they talk about are "bitches."

Time to go out back, I said. We gather around the small pond. One goon asks if the fish in the pond are real. I tell him that they are electric. He just nods. The grinning groom is dressed like the others, wearing huge black motorcycle boots with great studwork. One woman is wearing a V-neck tee-shirt, no bra, barefoot and her tattered jeans are dragging on the ground. She is the photographer. During the ceremony she stands on the outdoor furniture. She slipped and put her hand on my shoulder and then, for a second, on my head! The ceremony is over. They all clap and whistle real loud.

So now, how to get my well-earned pay. Rather than take two trips to ensure payment, I told her that I will give a few people a ride back to her place. As soon as those words came out of my mouth, goon one points to my car and says, "Is that your car?" I say yes, and he yells for all to hear that he is riding in the Benz. He and the uncle run for shotgun, Junior wins. A few minutes later the others are out in front of the house. Me, Junior and uncle are pulling out of the driveway. Walking along side, the photographer is snapping pictures like we are a limo carrying The Beatles.

Junior is posing big time. He asks if he can get a picture of him behind the wheel. I tell him no way that will happen. The uncle in the back says, "Let's go to a strip club!" I turn around and look at him and he shakes his head like "OK, OK?." I don't even respond to that one. I ask who the older lady is out front. He tells me that is his sister. I ask who the other girl was. The uncle says, "You ask too many questions, whada writin a book?"

I drive across town and across the tracks, pass the cemetery to the low rent district. Their humble abode is divided into four or five apartments. Their lot is a real mess. Next door is a chop shop of some kind.

The weirdos get out without saying a word. I wait in the car. The groom goes to get the money. All the wedding guests plus a few neighbors are sitting on the porch or mingling around. One woman with trashy good looks talks to me about how she wants to get rid of her husband. "I don't want him dead, just gone," she laughs. She asks me how she can do that. I tell her to file for divorce. She asks if that is something that I can do. No, I tell her, it is all up to her. She says bye and walks away. She is probably digging a hole in her backyard right now.

The money man comes out and fans the money like it's thousands of dollars. I didn't charge them much because I thought that it was going to be quick. I thank him, take the money and drive away.

The following morning I turned on the news and the big story in our town is, "Two people and a dog shot at wedding reception." I come to find out that the old lady at my house was shot along with some random guy. Their dog was shot twice. The out of town shooter got away, but everyone knew who he was. Over the next week the local news followed the condition of the dog, never mentioning the people. The dog owner cried on TV about how he had no way to pay for the medical expenses for his dog, so an anonymous donor stepped up and paid the bill.

I was telling a few high schoolers about this and one boy chimes in and says that he knows the people. He said that they stole the flowers for the wedding off the graves in the cemetery across the street from their house.

I'll meet you down by the river ...mañana

I made arrangements for a small wedding at a park along the Saugatuck River. The groom, Thomas, was a clean-cut professional man about 30 years old. He looked like the singer Jim Croce. Big bushy afro and a big thick moustache. He was marrying a South American woman that he had only known a short while. Make note.

The park is small, 5 acres on the river. Trees, tall grasses, rocks. A stone bridge one quarter mile upriver crosses over to a small downtown. It is picturesque for sure. This day is hot, uncomfortable. In attendance are 30 friends and relatives. They brought a few chairs for the elderly. The ceremony is set for 3:00. We are waiting for the bride and her maid of honor. Apparently, they are running late. At 3:20 she still has not arrived. The groom called her, and it went to voicemail. At 3:45 he asked me if I would wait a little longer. I told him that I will wait if he does. At 4:15 he asked me if he should wait much longer. I told him that it is entirely up to him. If he feels it in his heart, then he should wait. During this conversation I am keeping my eye on a very elderly woman sitting in the front row. I am wondering if she is dead. The temperature and her age are about the same, roughly 105.

At 4:50 a car pulled into the lot. The bride and her maid of honor got out and strolled over holding hands and laughing. This woman had us waiting in the heat for two hours and didn't say anything about it at all, nothing, no explanation nothing. After a lot of kissing and hellos we all gathered and got married. Afterwards I realized being late was in her culture. Being late didn't faze her a bit. I heard a few people mention the tardiness and she just laughed and blew it off. While waiting for her the groom stood in the heat patiently for nearly two hours, not knowing if she was going to show up. Later, someone said to the groom that he thought she was headed to the airport and back home. The groom didn't think that was funny but faked a smile.

This bride and the maid of honor would come to haunt me exactly one year later to the day.

It was the real Marilyn Monroe

I met a bride to be on a small pier here in my town to discuss her wedding plans. Her family had owned this little cove for many, many years. Her parents wanted to donate it to the town but city hall said no thanks. It is now the site of a private club owned and run by the locals. The wedding was to be out near one of the harbors on the other side of the Sound on Long Island in New York.

The woman, Diane, was in her 40's. She told me a very cool story. In 1962 she was about seven or eight years old. One afternoon she was playing exactly where we were standing now. She was playing with something or another here on the end of the short pier. She noticed a shadow come over her. She looked up but was blinded by the sun. She could tell that it was a woman. The woman asked, "hello, would you like a piece of candy?" The woman then began to dig in her purse. Diane stood up and saw that standing before her was Marilyn Monroe. "Here you go," Marilyn said handing her a piece of wrapped candy. Marilyn asked what she was doing and if she was having fun. Just then others came down the pier, Marilyn said goodbye and they all got into a small boat and shoved off. Diane waved goodbye as they headed away.

In sight, perhaps 3/4 of a mile offshore, sits Tavern Island. A beautiful 3 1/2 acre island once owned by Broadway producer/lyricist Billy Rose, friend of Marilyn Monroe. Billy would take guests out to the island for parties and weekend getaways. Diane happened to be in the right spot at the right time to meet one of the world's most beautiful and iconic women.

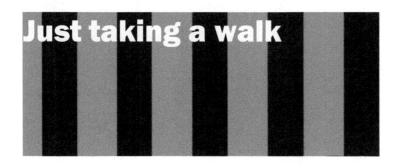

Just taking a walk

I was minding my own business walking my dog down my street. I see this guy walking toward me, and he is looking straight at me. He is wearing a fluorescent green mesh vest. He is clutching a book close to his chest. He gets closer and I see that he is special needs person. As he passes, and just to be friendly I say, "Nice vest." He stops and says, "Thank you, I'm 31 years old today." I tell him that's great and happy birthday. He says that it is not his birthday. He tells me that his birthday is Feb 8th, 1980. I ask if he lives nearby and he answers, "Yes, up the hill." I ask if he is married. And he says, "Yes," and he says it like a cheer. I then ask how long he has been married. He shouts "27 years!" "Boy, you married young," I say. He looks down and says, "Very young, goodbye," turns and walks away, the same way he came. I remind him that he was going the other way. Without turning around he yells back "I'm going in this direction now."

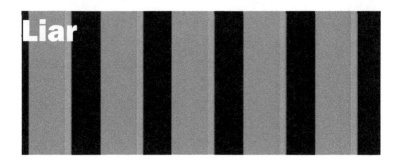

Liar

As I am driving to this ceremony, I say to myself that I will never accept a wedding that is this far away again. Two more exits and I will be in Rhode Island! This is one and a half hours' time from my home. It's so inconvenient when couples schedule a ceremony on a Friday at 5:00pm, peak driving time. I must leave way early to make sure that I get there on time. I do have a ceremony in Hammonasset Beach which is two exits back and another in Old Saybrook also in the area in the next few weeks. Too far.

When this bride booked the date about a month ago, she said that her fiancé was in the military. I told her that if she came to my home, I would marry them for free, to show my appreciation for the military. At that time I had two sons in Afghanistan. I do marry military free, but I asked her to come to the house because I didn't want to drive anywhere on a Friday at 5:00 P.M.. She said that they had a place already booked.

The venue was in Westbrook, CT at an upscale resort on Long Island Sound. I have done many ceremonies there. I arrived much too early. As I walked into the lobby, I saw the groom and the groomsmen hanging about drinking beer, like almost every wedding that I have been to. If there were an island or a forest where only groomsmen lived, they would always be aimlessly walking around bumping into each other with a beer in hand. I made small talk with them and I casually asked the groom which branch of the military he is in. He looked at me somewhat perplexed after the question and said that he is not in the military. He points to one guy and says that "he will be," points to another and says, "he was." I ask if he has ever been in the service. He says nope. Lots of thoughts in my head at that point. Bottom line is that the bride lied to me to get the ceremony for free. She most likely pulls this card from time to time. What am I going to do? I didn't make a big deal about it. She looks like a sleaze anyway.

Lieutenant Dan

I did a ceremony in N.Y. at a wedding factory along the Hudson River. A wedding factory is a venue that pumps out weddings and receptions, two, three, or four a day. I have been to dozens of these places all over the Northeast. They are mostly white plastic and white plaster.

This bride is shy and demure. The groom is from Brooklyn and is a "Hey wada ya sayyy" guy. He kept referring to me as Lieutenant Dan. He introduced me to everyone as Lieutenant Dan. Every time he would do this, he would punctuate it with a big laugh. I first smiled, then I smirked. I then thought, "OK, this is getting old." He kept with it.

In New York I am a licensed Minister, registered and licensed with the state. Most people think that I am a church going Minister guy. I could not be further from the pulpit. Everyone at this ceremony knew me as a Minister. The venue had a weird indoor setup. The couple and I stood in a gazebo type structure. The guests in the first row were about 40 feet away. Behind me was a very loud waterfall. It ran under a bridge, around in front of us and then into a pond. I had to almost yell to be heard. In the middle of the ceremony as I was yelling, the waterfall stopped. I simply said, "Oh thank you, Lord." It got a huge laugh.

While parking I saw an attractive woman in the parking lot chewing out her man, really on him. Later I saw them enter the room and she was walking ahead of him, still steaming. After the ceremony on my way out, I passed their table and I overheard her say, "Screw you." One thing I know for sure is there will be at least one couple having sex tonight and at least one couple who will not.

Linda and Bob and Lindsay and Rob

I did two weddings one day that were scheduled about 3 hours apart. I had done a few ceremonies close in time before. Usually it produces no problem.

Both ceremonies were small and at private homes. The first of the day, Linda and Bob, had about 6 or 7 guests. The second one, Lindsey and Rob's, had about 35 people. I remember Lindsey and Rob. They and their friends welcomed me. They were all like thinkers. The house was not far from my home. I believe that it was Lindsey's parent's place.

What made it interesting was that her father had worked for CBS Radio for many years. He was an interviewer. He had reel to reel tapes of most, if not all, of his work. He had interviews with the likes of, Amelia Earhart, Charles Lindbergh, Humphrey Bogart and up to early Bruce Springsteen. And I think he had Hitler as well! It was incredible! There were tape reels all in their original boxes on shelves in the living room. I touched them. A lot of history there. I tried to talk to him as much as possible, a very interesting man.

I had just come from performing Linda and Bob's wedding and I had their names fresh on my mind. Linda was pretty and from Colombia. Linda was wearing a very low-cut wedding gown. I thoroughly enjoyed my time standing before them but I could see so much breast that it was uncomfortable. I had the best seat in the house. I stood over her reading the vows from my black book. She was standing where my book almost touched her, where -as I was looking down - I could only see the book and her breasts. Just a little distraction. This is what people have done before. This is what this woman decided to wear to her wedding.

So I got to Lindsey and Rob's wedding. Bla, bla, bla, mingle, mingle. Showtime.

"We are gathered here today to join Linda and Bob in holy matrimony." In unison six people say, "*Lindsey and Rob*!." Oops, my bad. I called them by the wrong names. Sorry you video tapers. It was not a big deal to the couple. They were cool with it. They laughed and didn't give it another thought.

And neither did I.

Lost

This wedding was held on the border of Connecticut and Rhode Island, deep in the woods and at night. No phone services. I got lost three times. I saw a light off to my left, so I turned on the next dirt road. I drove about a 1/2 mile and turned left again toward the light. I see a large mansion and lots of cars. Odd setting in the middle of nowhere with no paved roads. This must be the place.

I was standing on the stairs with the six groomsmen. Suddenly, the guys come to attention. I look up and see the groom's mother at the top of the stairs. I could tell they fear her. She descends the stairs one at a time. I begin to fear her. At each step she adjusts a collar, a boutonnière, a button. When she gets to me, she adjusts my tie. She looked at me hard, with soulless black eyes. I swear I saw bats in her pupils.

The bride had a long exotic name with too many H's in it. I practiced pronouncing it all week. The groom's name was Jay, easy enough. When it came time for me to say her name in the ceremony, I nailed it! I turned to Jay and, for some mental lapse, I called him Eric. I had to stop. I told the guests that I tried ever so hard all week to learn her name and then ironically, I messed up his three-letter name. The guests just stared at me. Awkward. Man and wife yada, yada, I had an Amaretto Disoranno and headed back out into the lost.

Married in lingerie

I don't remember how this couple found me. On the phone the woman said that it would be just we three and she asked if I could make it Wednesday evening at 6:30. I did not meet them until that evening. The ceremony was at their condo across town.

I knocked and a handsome man about 40 opened the door and greeted me. He spoke with a heavy French accent. He was wearing nice leather loafers with no socks, slacks, a dark sports coat and a black turtleneck. We make small talk for a few minutes. He tells me that his fiancée is in the bedroom. After a few more minutes of talk he says to the other room, "Come on sweetheart, are you ready to do this?" No reply. Two or three minutes later she comes out. She has a youthful beautiful face, an hourglass figure and is wearing very sexy lingerie. Most specifically a skimpy red teddy. Hubby-to -be looks over at me and smiles. The bride says to me, "I have always wanted to get married in lingerie, is that OK, do you mind?" I didn't hear any of her words, and for a moment I was speechless.

Next to me the luckiest man on earth says, "I don't think he minds."

Marry us while we have sex

A guy called up and asked if I would do a ceremony for him and his fiancée. I said sure. He asked if I could do it this Friday. I told him that I could. He asked if I would perform the ceremony while they have sex. Immediately I wondered what his fiancée looked like. The guy was still asking, talking but I didn't hear him, I wasn't listening. My head was spinning. Can I do this? I'm sure that I can. There is no law that says that you must be wearing clothes at a wedding ceremony! Would it be OK if I brought a camera? I wondered what his fiancée looked like. I hear him say, "Massachusetts' '. In my head I hear the slamming of brakes, like in a cartoon. "Massachusetts, you live in Massachusetts?" "Yes, in Worcester," he says. In my mind I was already getting naked. I reluctantly told him that I was not licensed in the state of Massachusetts. He asked me why I was crying. I wondered what his fiancée looked like. I thought maybe they could come here to my house in Connecticut.

He said he was sorry that I couldn't do it. I told him, "Not as sorry as I am!" He laughed and hung up. I held the phone and wondered what his fiancée looked like.

Mob palace

I did a ceremony in the Bronx early one fall evening. Some parts of the Bronx are really beautiful, especially in that season. Wide neighborhood streets with big old houses and large aged trees down grass medians. The Bronx is about 45 minutes from my house.

This ceremony was not at a private residence. It was at a wedding factory. I came around the bend and found myself in front of the biggest, whitest, gaudiest, multi-columned building in the world. It took up the whole block. I did a ceremony in Queens for a friend at a place similar, but nowhere near as gargantuan. This was the wall from Skull Island, only it is white and in the Bronx.

I walk inside and the first thing I see are two massive staircases going up to the second floor, a staircase on each side of the room, Stairways to Heaven. There are hundreds of people here. The fur, the nails, the perfume. Many dead animals on the backs of these women. As I passed some women, their fragrance sucked up all the air in the immediate area and I had to gasp to stay alive. The men were mainly in tuxes, probably with many firearms hidden under those furs and tuxes. These were made men for sure. You respect them and they return that respect. One misstep, though, and you are wearing a cement kimono on the bottom of the East River at 111th Street.

A eunuch standing next to the stairs tells me that I am to go up to the left. Sure enough, at the bottom of the stairs there is a chain with a sign that says "Stairway to Heaven." I get upstairs and I see my crowd. It is the same as the crowd below, all fur, all dressed up. As we get ready to go in, I see that the waiters are having a difficult time herding the mob into the wedding hall. I suppose they don't like being told what to do.

I did meet up with the bride, her court and the groomsmen. We did not have a rehearsal and there were 14 bridesmaids and 12 groomsmen. It is going to be a little askew. The bride is wearing a wedding dress as big as a Buick. With the maid of honor I discuss how to lay out the bride's train once we reach that point.

We are all in position as the bride walks down the fur-lined aisle. This place is cavernous, and her dress fills half the room. She looks spectacular. She stands in her place next to me and the maid of honor begins spreading out the train. She is meticulously laying out every wrinkle and every bead. She keeps going with it and goes on and on. Finally I look at her and say in a very hush hush manner, "It's OK, that's good." She looks up at me with a nasty look and keeps going. I tell her again that it is fine. Finally the dress is to her satisfaction and the maid of honor steps back. She steps forward again and goes way out front and straightens something only she can see. The layout of the train is picture perfect. I look out at the couple, both very attractive, and see the dressed-up guests and the palace like room with its 50-foot ceiling. It looked like a Disney movie, and I was Goofy.

After the ceremony a man in his 60's about 5 ft tall, stops me and says, "Hey, that was good, you did good, ... and funny too." He pokes the side of his associate standing next to him, "This guy was funny." His sidekick doesn't want to commit so he just smiles. The guys continues with, "Show me anybody that doesn't think that this man was funny, I have ways of making them laugh." Leaning back and laughing he gives me a very mischievous look.

Yet another wedding where I must run for my life.

Mom and Dad hate each other

I have to start in the middle here because I don't remember anything about the couple or this wedding ceremony before the spectacle that was about to take place.

We are on a great lawn of a resort on the water in Connecticut. There are 150 seated guests as well as many passersby just hanging about the hotel grounds. Guests of the hotel are sitting at the outdoor bars, laying on the beach or just milling around.

The greaseball DJ starts the music. It is way too loud. Everyone within a mile put their fingers in their ears. Also, I worked the cues out with him earlier and he is not to start this particular song until I say, "Please rise for the bride." Since he jumped the gun on that I have to yell. The crowd looks toward the bride descending the steps. As the guests look away, I catch the DJ's attention. I motion that the music is too loud, but he waves me off! What a jerk. He's a weirdo, wearing all black, with a thin silver belt around his waist that is pulled in as tight as can be. He has a huge 80's big black curly mullet and he is dancing up a storm. I'll deal with him later.

The bride comes down the aisle, arm in arm with her father. They reach the correct spot in front of me and stop. The music fades and I say, "Who is it that gives this woman to this man?" Before the Dad can get it out, from the front row the bride's mother yells out "I do." Dad looks at me, pauses and says, "I do, your honor." Not to be outdone, the mother says, "I raised her, I am giving her away." I see Dad roll his eyes and he says something to himself very softly. Only then do I realize that the parents are not very fond of each other. The bride did tell me that her parents were divorced. What she didn't tell me was that her parents were also mortal enemies. The bride is almost in tears. The groom is staring at the ground. I see the guest's heads going back and forth like a crowd at a tennis match. The bride looks at me and I give her a little reassuring smile. I look out at the crowd and I say, "Anyone else?" The guests laugh. Dad laughs too. The bride smiles and I just plowed on through. It came off nicely in the end.

As I was leaving the bride thanked me and gave me a reassuring hug.

Mr. & Mrs. Inmate #4151730

A young woman of 25 called me and asked if I was available to officiate the wedding of her and her boyfriend. They have a two-year- old daughter and thought that it was time to get married. I asked where the ceremony would take place. She said it would be at the state penitentiary where he is doing 3-5. A child out of wedlock and Dad is in prison? He sounds like a great catch. At one point in our conversations over the next few weeks, I asked if he was innocent. She said no.

I was told to contact the warden's secretary who turned out to be from the community of the clueless. To get in I had to submit to a state background check as well as an F.B.I. check. I hoped that they didn't go back to the 60's. I knew that the statute of limitations was up on some things, so I wasn't too concerned. I get through the investigation process, so the wedding is a go.

The Big House is an hour and a half from my place. Normally I turn down requests from this far away, but I am doing it because the girl was having a hard time procuring an Officiant willing to go to jail. I didn't care, I had nearly been in a Mexican jail before. Me and some friends were arrested in Tijuana during Cinco De Mayo when I was about 17. The fat cop lined us up against the wall in front of the bar and went back inside to grab more partiers, so we just walked away.

My other reason for doing this was that I had never done a prison marriage before. I thought that it would look good for my background check at the gates of Heaven.

The day comes and it is raining. I walked into a holding cell right as I entered the front door. I am buzzed through 2 other cage doors. The guard is a cooperative guy. The bride is standing across the room. She radiates sweetness. We introduce ourselves. Her name is Rosa. A guard comes in with Inmate # 4151730, the groom. He is a short white man with glasses and tattoos and is wearing a khaki jumpsuit. Unique attire for his wedding day, I must say. I assume his suit was in the cleaners. We are ushered into a rec room. With a guard present I perform the ceremony. After I finish, I walk some feet away to give them a little privacy. I motion to the guard to give them some space. He barks out, "Nope."

They kiss again, the groom is searched and then escorted away to his cell. I walk out with the bride. Once you are out the door you can't re-enter. Her sister is supposed to be here to pick her up, but sis is nowhere is in sight. The bride has no phone, so she uses mine. Since we can't go back in and it is raining, we sit in my car. I must know so I ask her what her man is in for. She says that he got mixed up with the wrong people and that was really the problem. He was charged with aggravated assault, robbery, and possession of a deadly weapon. Maybe she doesn't see it, but I suspect what the problem is, and it's not his friends.

Musica and the dog run

I did a wedding for a friend of a semi-friend. The bride was an attractive pleasant woman in her 40's. The groom I don't remember much. The ceremony was going to be on their back deck. It was a bit windy and they wanted to do the Unity Candle ceremony. This is when the bride and groom each have a candle and together, they light a third, signifying two families and sets of friends blending into one. Again, it is windy, and the candles would not stay lit. During the ceremony a small crowd kept trying to light them. People kept lighting them as if they can light it better than the last person. At one point I did suggest that it might be because of the wind it was fruitless, but they kept at it.

Before we began, the bride brought me out back on the deck. I heard very loud Latino music. "And we have our musica," she said. It was so loud that I thought the speakers were under the deck or around the garage hidden somewhere. I thought it strange that they would be listening to cha cha. A woman standing nearby, and clearly irritated, said that the music was coming from over the fence. I look over it and sure enough I see an SUV with all five doors open. I can also see a bunch of people hanging out. The groom referred to them as renters. I wasn't having any of this. I headed out to the fence to have a nice word with these folks. Suddenly, halfway across the yard, the smell of dog poop hits me in the face, stops me dead in my tracks. I look around and the place is like a dog run. How could this guy live like this? How could this guy not pick it up, especially for his wedding?

I creep my way over to the fence and stand on a rock. I peek over and I see two guys hanging out. I wave for them to come over. One sees me for sure but ignores me. A pregnant woman holding a baby gets their attention and motions for them to go see what I want. Their cologne arrives well before they do. I told them that we are about to have a wedding ceremony and if they would please turn the music down for about 15 minutes. They look at each other, then they look back at me and then at each other again and then slowly back at me. Of course, they barely speak English. I look at them, stick my fingers in my ears, shake my head back and forth and say "Musica, musica." They look at each other and then back at me. A few silent seconds go by then they laugh, "OK, OK." One goes to the SUV and turns off the music. I say thank you and the other guy says, "15 minutes."

I gingerly walked back and did the ceremony. As I was leaving the bride handed me $50.00. It was a favor and I didn't want to charge them. I resisted but she stuffed it in my jacket pocket. She told me to spend it on fun.

Definition: The purpose of fun is to feel good and to maintain that feeling.

OK, I thought, I'll buy some weed.

My first time

This was the first ceremony I ever performed. Right after I booked it, I thought that I should have charged more because it was so far away. It was a cold, cold winter's day. What did I know, I was a rookie.

The town was so small that they shared the town hall with the neighboring town. No one here uses their blinkers because everyone knows where everyone else is going. The couple lived at a split in the road where an old abandoned barn/livery stable/gas station stood. Their place was above a garage 100 feet behind the barn. I parked and got out of my car and immediately slipped on the ice and down I go.

My first that I joined into holy matrimony were a young couple about 25 years old and they were kinda-sorta in love. The groom was assigned to submarine duty in nearby New London. The bride was a Navy fighter pilot in training.

Present were the bride's skinny best friend and best man, the exact double for Garth Brooks. Short and stocky, jeans, western shirt, big black hat and a thick drawl. A good ol' boy. Also, in attendance was a large, ugly, smelly dog that would not stop slobbering on me. The whole time I was there this dog was on me, drooling. The bride tried to get it to stop but it was useless.

It just leaned on me and with big sad eyes. I couldn't be too upset with that!

Everything went fine. I did my magic, they kissed and that was that. I sat down in the little kitchen to sign the license. Garth came over to me and asked if I would like to smoke a joint out on the deck. I politely declined the invitation. I left, and on my way out slipped once again on the ice at the bottom of the stairs.

Mystic

I drove to Mystic, Connecticut to marry Todd and Juliette. I have done five or more ceremonies in Mystic Seaport. The seaport is a restored old New England whaling village. The village of Mystic was founded in 1654 and quickly rose to prominence as a shipbuilding center during the clipper ship era. Mystic is located within the town of Stonington. Stonington is the only Connecticut town facing the Atlantic Ocean. All the other towns face Long Island Sound. The town is steeped in history as a whaling port and now the home to one of the last remaining commercial fishing fleets in the state. It has many beautiful large 19th century homes built by mariners. Captain Nathaniel B. Palmer, discoverer of Antarctica made Stoneington his home. Even bigger than Antarctica is that the movie *Mystic Pizza* with Julia Roberts was made here.

I was waiting in the mist on a bench on a dirt road in the village. The groom appears out of nowhere. This is our first face to face meeting. We talked a bit and I asked him for the marriage license. As he stands, he pulls an envelope out of his breast pocket and hands it to me. He says see you later and walks down the road. I open the envelope and it is a $2000.00 check made out to no one. Nice tip! At that moment a limo pulls up and the bridal party rolls out. We are supposed to meet in the block-long old rope-making building just behind me. We do a short rehearsal. A little girl falls backwards over a bench and starts crying and doesn't stop, even as the ceremony begins.

The groom enters. I greet him with the envelope. I say thanks for the tip, but it is too much. He breaks out with a big sigh of relief. The check is for the overpaid DJ. The DJ was late, and he can't get it together. The ceremony was on a little grass outcropping in the harbor. It was lightly raining. The DJ could not get power for his system, so we all stood around waiting for him. I told him my last words, which is his cue to start the recession song. Of course he started the music before I had finished speaking.

Upon leaving, I had to interrupt the photo shoot to say goodbye. The groom fumbles for his wallet and pulls out all the bills and hands them to me. I tell him that it is not necessary, and he shoves the wad into my hand and says, "Thanks, it was perfect." I put the cash in my pocket and head out.

When I get to my car, I count it out. When I get to 16 I stop. I stopped because that is all there was, 16 dollars.

New Year's Eve

I got a last-minute call from Senena who was calling on behalf of her very distraught friend. Her friend, the bride, was so shook up that she could hardly speak. So Senena stepped up. It seems that her officiant had just bailed. The ceremony was to be held at the Ritz-Carlton in New York in just three days' time.

The groom informed me that they were, in fact, already married. His family and the guests are not aware of this minor fact and they wanted to keep it that way. I have done this many, many times. A couple is already secretly married but still want a big wedding for their family. I told him that it would be a surcharge for me to keep that little tidbit quiet. I was kidding, of course.

I wore a black pinstriped suit. When I walked in, I saw that it is black tie, all tuxedos. I meet the handsome groom and his fake pneumatic bride. She wore a very low-cut revealing gown. I didn't talk to her after that because she was so shy. I did the ceremony.

I stayed for about 45 minutes after the ceremony. I had never seen so many food stations, a different one in each room off the main ballroom. The food looked and was superb. Each room had a giant ice sculpture. I made the rounds and tried a little something in each room.

I was strolling about in one of the rooms. I happen to walk up to a circle of about 8 men. They were each drinking and having a good time. I saw a few big pinky rings. The gentleman I happen to stand next to wore an impressive one and was five and a half feet tall and five and a half feet wide. The very second I walked up they all stopped talking and stared at me. The man says, "Can I help you?" I am already backing up. I raise my drink, smile and slowly back away, thinking that now is a good time to leave. I don't say anything to anyone. I get my coat and beat it.

Outside it was snowing, and I made it out alive.

Leaving like I was never there is getting to be an art form with these kinds of weddings.

New York Bush People

I married a couple up near Poughkeepsie. The house was on a cliff overlooking junk on a hillside. Of course the couple were amiable, as most are on their wedding day. The bride was in total charge. The groom was a real wisenheimer. Nothing that he said was remotely funny. The only funny thing about him was that he looked like a big square cardboard box. I get to the house. The front door is about three feet from the road. The ceremony will be in the living room. When I enter the place, there are five teenage girls and the same number of guys all standing in the messy living room. They were the bridal party. I don't know why they acted so formal because we were just in the living room and they all were dressed kind of sloppy, shorts, tank tops, jeans, a Jets tee-shirt. Dad was sitting in the kitchen, dining, living room area, I asked for the marriage license. They don't have it. Evidently there is a problem with the application. The bride began to tell a long story about the trouble they are having getting a marriage license. I tell them that I cannot marry them without a marriage license.

Skip to 2 months later. They call and they now have the license. They say that they will come to my house. I tell them we cannot do that because the license was issued in New York and by law I must marry them in the state of New York. I told them that if they had a license issued in my town in Connecticut, I would marry them at no charge. If I had to come to them then, and since it is way up the Hudson River, I will have to charge them again, but it would only be half price. It is not saying words, it is suiting up, driving for an hour, gas, etc. I get there and we do the ceremony. Afterward I wandered out on the balcony/deck overlooking the ravine. I look over the rail and I see that the hillside is dotted with, among other things, an old boat hull, a refrigerator, a car hood and two ten-year-old scavengers turning things over. The guy cleaning the grill asks me if I am staying for hamburgers. He shoos off a cat that has been sitting on the grill. He tosses off empty beer cans, an old plate with a big bone on it, a can of Turtle Wax and a bunch of twigs and leaves. I asked him when the last time that he used this grill. He said that it wasn't too long ago.

Passing through the living room on my way out, I notice a young girl sitting alone on the couch. She was not here earlier. I estimate she is 14 years old. She is strikingly pretty, wearing the shortest of short shorts and a small sleeveless top. She has cupid bow lips with bright red stripper lipstick.

She is Lolita. I feel sorry for her looking so pretty here in the backwoods. Bright red lipstick and short shorts? She knows exactly what's up.

One minute in Paris

I was in Paris on a warm July night. It was around 11:30 and I was sitting at a sidewalk café drinking what turned out to be a $12.00 glass of Coke. Nancy had gone inside for a minute.

As I sat there, a couple came scurrying by with a real purpose. He was holding a bouquet and wearing a suit with no tie. She was wearing a white, sleeveless, short mini dress with a long wedding veil that was flowing in the wind as they ran by. For an instant I was living in a 1940's black and white French postcard. As quickly as they appeared from the right, they disappeared to the left, down the cobblestone street and into the Parisian night. A great visual that can only be had at a sidewalk café late at night in Paris.

Paddy married a bitch

I did a wedding for a young couple at an upscale Italian restaurant and wedding factory on the water in New Haven. They were in their 20's. This was one of those weddings in which no one spoke to me. I tried to engage in a few conversations, but people were just not interested.

The ceremony was performed a few feet from the water in a gazebo which sat on a large well-manicured lawn overlooking the harbor. A picturesque setting.

The couple had chosen vows and all the paperwork that I had seen stated the groom's name as Michael. Family and friends gather, and I begin. "We are gathered here today to join, [whatever her name was] and Michael." Right then she pipes in "Paddy." This is the first time I have heard the name Paddy in all the preparations. "His name is Paddy," she says softly yet sternly. I look down in the vows and see the name Michael written about one hundred times. Normally I have about a page or a page and a half to read. The vows that she had given me were about 4-5 pages in length. I got it right most of the time, however I missed it two or three times and she corrected me each time and each time she got a little more heated. I thought for sure she was going to knock me out! At one point with clenched teeth, from the front row, her mother yelled at her to stop.

Michael - I mean Paddy - got a chuckle out of it. I thought so too, but the bride sure didn't!

She sprung the name change on me at the last minute. Well, now I have a better name for *her*.

Pulpit fiction

I didn't meet this couple before the wedding, no rehearsal. I met them the day of the ceremony at the venue. The bride had flaming dyed orange-red-blue hair. She looked like a lit match. The groom was rude straight out of the gate. Both were plump and tatted up to the max. He a little more than her. They were bikers. The guests arrive and they are all bikers. Most of them tried to dress up but it wasn't pretty. There was a lot of sleevelessness going on. This was a decent wedding venue. I had been there numerous times. This picture was like oil and water. It just didn't mix, flannel, denim, jeans, and boots in a big pink building.

The venue representative told me that last week, at the hotel across the street, the father of a bride had died while taking a shower just before the ceremony. They went on with the wedding.

This ceremony went well, no deaths while I was there. I mingled with a biker and some biker chicks. They were all cool. I told them that my Dad had a bike his whole life.

These bikers didn't intimidate me. My conversations with the couple were good and I gave my usual casual ceremony, which they had picked out, and they seemed to enjoy themselves.

A week later I see a review from the groom on a wedding website. All my reviews are 5 out of 5. He gave me a 3. He wrote that I could have been more professional. He perceives professional differently. He had a shaved head, a beard, 8000 tattoos, and multiple piercings. He acted rude for the whole ceremony. You would think by his lifestyle and his outlaw boundaries he would be more liberal in his thinking.

Make my day, Chump.

Really big shoes

A young woman called and set up a wedding at her father's house. It was just past an old cemetery around the corner from my place.

The woman was in her thirties, attractive and well spoken. She worked for an insurance company. I didn't meet her husband-to-be until the day of. The ceremony was held in her father's back yard. On the patio they had a tent cover over a small bar, up some stone steps on a slope that is their yard. It was a good day for a wedding.

I saw the groom for the first time out front. I wasn't introduced but after years of doing this I can tell who the groom is from a mile away. Most of the time the groom looks like deer in the headlights. Wide eyed and not knowing which way to go. Few are cool, calm and collected. Many immediately look for the bar or already have a drink in hand when they arrive. This is true whether the event is large or small. With most of the large posh ceremonies whether it is a country club or a multimillion-dollar estate, the guys in the wedding party almost always arrive in the limo drinking. At the rehearsal they are most always smashed, some pleasantly, some not so much.

I am out front of the house and I see the groom getting out of a car on the other side of the street. He's sporting a new suit, and he's well- groomed. When the car pulled away, I saw that his shoes were enormous. I mean waaay big! He walked toward me. He walked up the steps. Funny got funnier. Someone introduced us and told me that he doesn't speak or understand English, he speaks Spanish. He has a typical Hispanic name, Norman.

This makes my job here more difficult. The wife speaks English and Spanish. As I am talking to this guy, I can see he is smiling and his head is going around in little circles and he is wearing the big, big shoes. I am reasonably sure that he did not wear these shoes to look like a clown. For some reason they were probably all he could find. Maybe this big shoe thing is all the rage back home. I see him a few times standing by the big tree or walking by. No one ever mentioned his shoes.

We all get together ready to start. I begin doing the voodoo. I read vows from a small book. I look down and usually keep my eyes on my book. But in this case, I see below the book and the tops of his huge shoes on the ground. I can barely control myself. He was coached to say yes at the appropriate times. As soon as I pronounced them the music began, and the party started.

I wandered over to the bar and started to make small talk with the Rasta bartender. He wasn't into conversation. I asked for a Sprite. He asked if I wanted a glass and I said of course. He gave me a dirty look. He was doing this gig grudgingly.

Just before I left, I was watching the groom and admiring his big, big shoes. Seriously, the shoes were enormous. I pictured him spinning these big, big shoes really fast like a helicopter in a cartoon and taking off over the tops of the trees and into the clouds.

Can you give us a minute?

I did a ceremony yesterday here at my home. They called, and we set up a time for a short ceremony for the coming Thursday night.

Thursday came and the couple arrived and pulled their car around back behind my house. They proceed to sit there. After about ten minutes or so they got out and came up to the door. It was a fair dinkum day and I asked them if they would like to say their vows next to the waterfall and pond here in the yard. The bride could not make up her mind. They went back and forth a few times, so I suggested we go in the house. I went over the license and all was in order. I positioned us under a stained-glass window in an alcove on one side of my living room. I ask if they have rings, which is the moment when things go a little off. They hesitate and then say no. I tell them I have a short set of vows. Simple and sweet as the groom suggested. Before I can utter the first word, the bride stops me. "Can we have a minute... alone?" she says. I thought this babe has changed her mind. I say sure and I left the room.

15 long minutes later the groom opened the door and said that they would just like for me to sign the license and then they would leave. I came into the room and sat on the couch across from them. I explained that legally I must ask each if they want to marry the other. They said "OK." I then said, "Do you Shelia want to marry Orlando?" She said yes. I then repeated the same

for him and closed with, "I pronounce you man and wife." They smiled and said thank you and left.

I can't help but wonder what that was all about. I wonder if they are still married.

Shelter from the storm

For many years my wife and I worked as volunteers at the local annual Oyster Festival. This once a year deal has rides, craft booths and lots of New England food. Topping each night is a concert with well-known acts. One particular day I happened to have a wedding just across the harbor.

I arrived at the beach club for the wedding and as rain was expected they had two giant tents set up. There were at least 100 guests under the tents and spreading out on the lawn. It started to get windy. We did the ceremony out on the lawn near the water with more wind. I said good luck, goodbye, and I left.

I went home to change out of my suit. It took 15 minutes to get to my house and back to the harbor. By the time I got to the festival the sky was turning dark. I made it to my booth at the front gate. Nancy was there waiting. It is hard to put into words what happened next so I will let Mark Twain do that:

"Directly it began to rain, and it rained like all fury, too, and I never saw the wind blow so. It was one of these regular summer storms. It would get so dark that it looked all blue-black outside, and lovely; and the rain would thrash along by so thick that the trees off a little ways looked dim and spider-webby; and here would come a blast of wind that would bend the trees down and turn up the pale underside of the leaves; and then a perfect ripper of a gust would follow along and set the branches to tossing their arms as if they was just wild; and next, when it was just about the bluest and blackest- fst! it was as bright as glory and you'd have a little glimpse of tree-tops a-

plunging about, away off yonder in the storm, hundreds of yards further than you could see before; dark as sin again in a second, and now you'd hear the thunder let go with an awful crash and then go rumbling, grumbling, tumbling down the sky towards the underside of the world, like rolling empty barrels down stairs, where it's long stairs.

- excerpted from Huckleberry Finn

As I stood at the gate undercover, I looked across the field and saw people running for cover. The wind had picked up fast. I looked across the harbor where I had just performed the wedding ceremony. I saw the two large tents fly up and sail on through the sky. It was surreal. The storm lasted about 20 minutes and then the sun came out. Typical New England weather. As the old joke goes, if you don't like New England weather just wait five minutes.

I called the bride the next day to see if all was well. She told me most everyone made it to the changing rooms or at least under the overhang when the storm hit. No one was hurt, the food was saved. And they danced under the stars. Just like being married on the Titanic.

Shorties

I performed at another Red Barn event. The groom never stops smiling. He had this big infectious smile. I am sure that everyone who sees this grin can't help but grin too. He has probably caused a million smiles without ever saying a word. What a great gift the man has. His name was Benjamin Franklin. Imagine going through life with a name like that, wow! Why did his parents do that to him?

It was our great statesman, inventor, and author Benjamin Franklin who said, "Marriage is the most natural state of man and... the state in which you will find solid happiness." He also said, "Keep your eyes wide open before marriage and ...half shut afterwards."

****

I did a quickie for a young couple. A sweet little ceremony in their condo just a few minutes from my house. Her parents were there, up from New Jersey. The groom was short, and the bride was very pretty. She was also VERY pregnant. Her due date was this very day. The husband turned out to be very sensitive and emotional. He started crying right when I started the vows and got more blubbery as we went on. I was going to send him to his room if he didn't stop.

****

After a ceremony, I was walking through the reception. I walked into a circle of men talking. Many of the men at this wedding were weightlifters. You can tell by the necks. I looked at them and said, "Anyone want to wrestle?" Out of nowhere a hunched over 200 year old man said, "I'll wrestle you." We all laughed. Not more than 10 minutes later I saw that old cat asleep in a corner chair.

****

At a wedding at a country club, I was in the dressing room with a bride and her court. I asked her for the marriage license. She said, "I thought you had it!" "Why would I have it?" I replied. She told me that the officiant is supposed to get the marriage license. I had mentioned in our initial meeting and subsequent emails what the process was for getting a marriage license. She flew into a rage saying she can't get married today, someone go get my fiancé, where is my mom? She was in full wedding dress regalia, a big veiled snowball bouncing off the walls. I stood back, let it flow and told her to settle down. I explained that we can have the ceremony today as planned and next week she should get the license and then come to my home and I would marry them, and all would be well again in crazytown. She agreed. It didn't turn out well though. I ran over a rabbit on my way out.

****

Just before a ceremony in New York, the groom tells me that we will be one bridesmaid short. He then says with a cat's grin, "Do you want to know why?" I said that I was very intrigued. "She checked herself into a mental institution this morning."

****

A woman called yesterday. She was drunk. She made arrangements for a brief ceremony at my home for Monday morning. She laughed a lot on the phone. After finalizing everything I told her not to forget to bring her fiancé. She said "Who?" laughed wildly and hung up. They showed up on time, 10am. They were in their 40's, both smoking. I tell them no smoking please at my house. They apologize and quickly put the butts in their car. They were very, very tipsy. The first thing they asked me was if there was an open bar nearby. He was wearing jeans and a jacket. She was in a blouse and skirt with very high heels. I commented on her shoes. Her reply was that Larry likes this kind of pumps, so you know what's going to happen later." She laughed drunkenly. I looked at Larry and he was checking for something in his wallet and without lifting his head he smiled and nodded his head up and down in total agreement.

****

At a very classy hotel in Stamford, CT after the ceremony, I was standing at the buffet table. There were many different kinds of food and I was hungry. I casually picked up an olive and popped it into my mouth. It lodged in my throat, I choked, and the olive quickly shot out and landed in a bowl of dip. A girl about 11 or 12 years old was sitting nearby and saw this happen. I looked at her, she gave a thumbs up.

****

We are all standing in our positions at a rehearsal. The groom, best man, and bride have yet to come out. I am standing next to one of the groomsmen. He is tall and rigid, sporting a military style haircut. He is wearing wraparound dark sunglasses. I casually say to him, "You're going to lose the shades, right?" Without moving an inch he says, "That's not going to happen."

Later the bride points out her family to me. As it turns out the guy with the shades is her brother. He is a Secret Service agent assigned to the White House. She says that he probably wears his sunglasses while he sleeps. I think he is watching us. I can't tell with the shades. We are indoors. She says that he needs to take off the sunglasses for the ceremony. As I leave, I say goodbye passing him on the way out. He nods. The next day at the wedding he is not wearing the shades and has big beautiful brown eyes.

****

I was standing waiting for the light to change at 86th and 3rd in New York City, 3 blocks from my old apartment. From behind me comes 3 or 4 adults and 20 children holding hands. My educated guess was that the kids are about 6 or 7 years old. I look at the young teachers and smile. One little girl looks at me and says, "Why aren't you at work?" I say that I am working. She says, "It doesn't look like you're working." I told her that I marry people and I had just married a couple in Central Park. Another little girl asks, "How old are they?" I say that they are about your teacher's age. A teacher listening, smiles. One boy asks if they were boys or girls. The second girl looks at the boy and says that boys can't marry boys. I say they were a boy and a girl. Another girl chimes in with "Girls can't marry girls," and then adds, "You can't have two moms." The first girl says, "Yes you can, (points) Dakota has two moms and I saw them kiss." Lots of ooooooh's.

Snow whites

I performed a civil ceremony for two women just down the street at the gazebo on Town Green. The ladies came up from New York City. It was December and there was snow on the ground. They both came dressed in all white winter wear. Fur hats, gloves, scarves and knee-high boots, all white. Via IVF one was very pregnant. Also along for the nuptials was their photographer, dressed in all black. She looked inconsistent in the all-white surroundings. We did the ceremony in the gazebo on the Green. The 300-year-old Saint Paul's Church is just across the street, so we went over there to take more pictures. It was a cozy and intimate ceremony. They insisted that I pose with them for the pictures.

A month or so later I got a package in the mail from the girls. Inside I find a grateful note thanking me for a beautiful ceremony and being so progressive in my views of marriage. There was a box inside as well. My first thought was, "Alright, cookies!" It was a book. It was a hardbound book of pictures from the ceremony. Hard pages with cutouts for the pictures with a plastic covering over them, very classy. The pictures of them were beautiful. White fur hats with pretty faces in an all-white background. While I never photograph well, I appreciated the book and the unexpected thought.

So I said the wrong thing

A guy set up a small ceremony to be held at his home about a mile from my place. I got there and they were ready to go. They were a couple in their early 50's. The groom's 20-year-old son was there to videotape the event. They had picked out vows from what I had sent them.

We took our places and I began. I have read these same vows 100 times or more. There is a verse that says, "To make your marriage work, it will take trust." Well, I messed up and said, "It will take *lust*." As soon as I said this, which I thought was a minor comical error, the bride had a fit. The groom and his son just laughed. She huffed and puffed and walked in circles. The groom had to calm her and bring her back around. I looked at the son and he gave me the OK sign. I asked her if she would like me to do it again. She swiftly said no. I felt bad, as it obviously meant a lot to her and I messed it up. I apologized.

On the other hand, this is your 3rd marriage, girlfriend. By now you may have noticed that stuff happens.

Somewhere in time

Another nuptials way too far from my home. About one-and one-half hours' time. Woodstock, Connecticut, farms, cows, horses, corn and fields and not much else on either side of the road. It is up in the top right-hand corner of the state, 5 miles from the Mass border and way too far.

I finally arrived. The location for the ceremony is an historic farm built in the early 1700's, turned B&B. It has a garden in the side yard where the ceremony will take place. I noticed old style Root Beer chilling in a large washtub. All the flowers and trimmings were handmade. Out of the side door steps a man in a white shirt and vest, he works here. He looks like he has stepped out of the root beer label. Guests file into the garden. They are all dressed in period clothing, 1800's. The groom calls to me from the second-floor window. He is waving a handkerchief like a woman on a train. His wife to be, a dainty little thing, tries to poke her head out but bangs it hard on the window. She puts her hand on her head and disappears back inside.

I went up to see how they wanted the ceremony to play out. I step in the room and I find they too are in vintage clothing. I tell them that I didn't get the memo about the attire. They said that they don't think that they told me. I ask about her head. She says that it hit hard, and she was dizzy for a minute or so. I ask her how many fingers I have up. I keep changing from four to two to three. She says twelve.

We lined up in the hall ready to go. As we begin to walk, I notice a hat rack next to the door. Hanging on the rack is a top hat. As we pass by, I grab the top hat and put it on. Now I feel that I belong!

The ceremony went well. I looked out over the guests and felt as though I was in a Twilight Zone episode. I pronounced them husband and wife and they went back down the aisle while their guests showered them with flower petals, spices and what looked like twigs.

Suddenly the top hat was abruptly lifted from my head. A munchkin of a woman stood there and said, "This is a museum piece and not for use!" I apologized.

The bride and groom insisted that I take a watermelon home with me.

Staten Island fiasco

I was at a car dealer in California with my son when I got a call from a crazy woman in Staten Island. She wanted to get married at her mom's home, no friends, no frills, no nothing. Hoping she would refuse I gave her an outrageous price and she accepted. We talked, set the time and place and said our goodbyes. One minute later I get a ping on my phone and she has paid. Another minute goes by and she calls to change the day. She now wants to have the ceremony early in the morning on New Year's Day. We renegotiate and finalize.

As soon as I got off the plane, a message from her arrives and she wants to change the time from morning to evening. I tell her that it's not possible. They say that they are in Massachusetts and can't be back in New York until 11:00 A.M. Since I didn't want to get up early anyway, I tell her that works.

I had planned to take the Staten Island Ferry from Manhattan but didn't find out until I was a few blocks away that since 9/11 the ferry doesn't take cars. So I cross the Brooklyn Bridge into Brooklyn and get on the Verrazzano Narrows Bridge, then cross over to Staten Island. I have been through here on the turnpike but never into the interior of Staten Island. I had always pictured the island as a Detroit sort of place. It has seen better times. Staten Island has many reputable middle class neighborhoods and many million-dollar homes. Beautiful nature preserves as well. Todt Hill is the highest elevation on the east coastal plain from Florida to Cape Cod.

I pulled into their neighborhood and noticed is that there are homes on the right and no homes on the left. You can see all the way to the Atlantic Ocean about a half mile away. The houses on the left were wiped out by a recent hurricane.

I get to their house, and it is in bad shape due to the storm. I knock on the door and the mother greets me. A plump woman in her 40's. On the couch is her disabled 16-year old son. He has a form of Tourette's Syndrome so he has outbursts. Her daughter and her fiancé are not there. Mom tells me that they are out running errands. Time passes. An hour goes by. They have no cell phone. I go outside to contemplate. Finally they pull up. They get out of a sad car. She is wearing a crushed blue velvet two-piece jogging outfit and gigantic sunglasses. The groom is dressed like a mechanic. I look around for the cameras.

We all went into the house. I went into the kitchen and said something to the effect of, "Let's do this." The girl said, "Just sign it, please." I look at the dude and it becomes clear that these two have not been seeing eye to eye for this morning. I make it as quick as possible. I asked if each wanted to marry the other. They both said yes, and I said, "You're married."

As I gathered up the paperwork the mother asked me to come into the other room. She led me into her back bedroom. The first thing I saw was a giant picture on the wall of a man in a military uniform. "Who is that?" I asked. "That's my husband. He's dead," she said. It turns out that she is a paralegal. She gave me her card. She asked if I would be interested in marrying people that she sends me. I asked if this was an immigration thing. She explained that people come to her looking for permanent resident status. One way to obtain that is through marriage. I thought that this was my big opportunity to get into human trafficking. I told her that I didn't think that it would work for me. Which is not what she wanted to hear, so she quickly escorted me out. As I crossed the living room the boy on the couch put something behind his back real quick. I left.

The three hour late guy

A young woman called and set up a wedding at a vineyard in New York. I didn't meet her and her fiancé until the day of the ceremony. The time for the ceremony was set for 5:00 P.M. I arrived at 4:20.

The bride and her "gang" are hanging out in the restroom of a small converted barn. It gets close to 5:00 and the groom has yet to appear. I go to talk to the bride, and I am stopped by an enormous woman in a 3rd grader's fluffy pink dress. "She can't see you right now." I explain that it will only take a second. She grudgingly disappears. I wait outside patiently. The bride's father comes over and starts a conversation with me, a humble man, very pleasant. He is from Colombia and has come to New York for his daughter's wedding. He tells me that he has five daughters.

About 15 minutes later a new woman comes out. I take a step toward her, she sees me and turns and darts back into the restroom. It is now 5:00. A minute or so later the big chiffon girl returns and says that the bride can talk now. She opens the door. The bride is just pulling up her dress. The little room is packed with ladies, more chiffon, choking perfume, hairspray and general wedding paraphernalia. I barely have a foot in the door. I ask a few questions about the ceremony. One of her lieutenants answered most of my questions. I ask about the groom. The lady closest to the door opens it and says," He will be here, now you have to go." I go out and hang out on the deck, this certainly is not the first time a wedding ceremony has started late. At 5:30 I ask one of the ladies about the groom. Without breaking stride in her walk she reveals that he is late. Everyone central to the wedding is in that restroom. The guests mill about outside.

6:00 comes and it has turned dark. I knock on the restroom door and it opens a crack. The lady sees that it is me and opens wider. The bride says that the groom is running late and is on his way. She says that they live nearby so it won't be long. I smile and say OK. The door shuts right on my face. A half hour later a lady comes out to get a can of soda. She looks at me and says that he is on his way.

At 7:00 I again knock on the door. It opens, I peek in and I see that the bride is upset. I asked her what she would like to do. She did and didn't answer in the same sentence. "I don't know - wait?"

Hector the groom did show up at 8pm. In a powder blue three-piece suit, no tie, white shoes. I met him near the parking lot, and as we walked, I asked him about being late. "I don't know man, I don't know," is all that he would say. This guy made it abundantly clear that he was having second thoughts.

The ceremony was set up in the vineyards for a daylight event. It is now a spooky dark event in those vineyards. There were no lights, but she insisted. I had a young boy hold a flashlight over my shoulder so I could read the vows. Babies were yelling and crying.

It was over and as everyone walked out I hesitated with the couple for a moment. Holding hands facing me but looking down, they apologized and together as if on cue, they exited stage right. I paused with my thoughts, and then I exited stage left.

What a day for them to remember. If they stay married, I am sure they will eventually tell stories and laugh about it. But I wasn't laughing.

The bride and her maid of honor are back

I answer my ringing phone. It is the bridesmaid of the difficult woman that I had married last year, the woman who was two hours late for her own wedding. The bridesmaid is now getting married and wants me to perform her ceremony. The bride from last year is now the bridesmaid.

The rehearsal and ceremony were at an old historical restaurant in Westport called The Red Barn. I found out at the rehearsal that the groom does not speak English. He is a handsome man who seems perpetually happy. Perhaps it's due to the visible bump on his head. At the rehearsal, standing at the altar in the gazebo, the groom pulls out a piece of paper. The bride-to-be tells me that he wants to read this, in Spanish, right after saying his vows. I will nod to him when it is time for him to read.

In a repeat of her friend's wedding last year, come wedding day, the bride is late, significantly more than an hour. While waiting, I tried to have a conversation with the groom, but alas he understood little of what I was saying. The bride did arrive at one point but once she realized that the photographer was not there to take her picture she promptly got back into the limo and the car drove off. It was another half hour before she returned. The couple stroll in and act like nothing had happened, just like last year. No apologies to me, her friends or family, nothing said. 15 minutes of minor commotion and then we began.

I say what I say, and the groom fumbles with "I do." It is now time for his speech. I nod to him. Without the notes he begins to speak, in English. He proclaims his undying love and lifelong commitment to his new bride in such a heartwarming and loving way that she begins to cry. It was a very, very moving moment. This guy learned these words in English this past week so that he could say them to her in English. He said them in such a meaningful way that you could tell that it was coming from deep within his soul. It was quite an experience to witness real honest true love. That moment when they were looking in each other's eyes was made in heaven.

After the vows I watched a girl-on-girl argument conducted in Spanish, waited for a break then I beat it out of there.

The Kommisar

A very decisive woman picked a set of vows for her ceremony. I always mention the closing words to them beforehand, "You may kiss YOUR bride." I am not a fan of this. It is chauvinistic and implies ownership. I suggest "You may kiss," and maybe add "for the first time as husband and wife." You need to start off on a level playing field. I explain this to this bride-to-be who is foreign born, nasty, stern, firm as a riding crop and not at all afraid to use it. The couple said that they would think about the ending and get back to me. The wedding was six months away. She calls a few months later. "Kiss the bride" is what she wants. I put it in the notes.

The day arrives. Before the ceremony I go to see her in the bridal suite. She sees me but does not say a word. She goes into the bathroom and shuts the door. At that moment the photographer spins me around and starts throwing questions at me. He is about 4 feet tall and is carrying a small step ladder. The groom is drinking beer in the hallway.

Cut to the ceremony. Me and the groom are standing before the guests waiting for her to come down the aisle. She arrives at her position and says under her breath, "Say, *your bride*." Talk about last minute changes! I read for 10 minutes and I get to the end and automatically I read what has been written, "You may kiss *the* bride." She yells, "YOUR BRIDE, I told you to say "your bride!" I was so very embarrassed. Then I see that the crowd is sitting there smiling, frozen in time. Then I remember the groom telling me that being German, none of the guests, not one, speaks or understands English.

Even from her tone the guests didn't suspect anything was odd. They all sat there smiling.

The bride went upstairs to freshen up. So I sprint to the groom to say goodbye and then exit. The groom complimented me and said what a great job I had done. I got the feeling that he couldn't have cared any less. He was married and he was having a good time. At least for the moment, until he feels that riding crop upside his head.

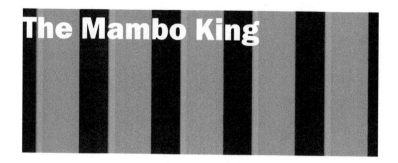

The Mambo King

A woman called and booked a wedding here at my house. We emailed back and forth too many times and she also called too many times. Each and every time that she talked to me or emailed me, she told me how great it was to find me. I was a perfect match for their personalities. I never got the connection. She must have told me 1000 times, even when we were walking out at the ceremony and 10 times after that.

She was a woman around 50 and this was her first marriage. The groom told me that he was 56 years old. He was the epitome of a Mambo King. He stood about 5'5" tall, 120 lbs., had jet black hair, greased back. He was wearing a Miami type outfit, very clean, but a few sizes too big. He had lots of bling. I saw a gold anklet on the outside of his socks. His elderly mother was the only guest. She seemed to be asleep most of the time.

I read the ceremony and they read something to each other. She spoke of finally finding her soulmate and she knows they will be happy for the rest of their lives. She cried.

After they had left, I was signing the license. Under her name one question was 'number of this marriage.' 1 was her answer. I looked under the Mambo King's name where it said 'number of this marriage.' 6 was his answer.

The most expensive by far

A young couple from Manhattan came to my home to work out the details of their wedding. The ceremony was going to be at the groom's parent's home in Westport, about 3 miles from my place. I was told to park in the lot they rented next to the train station and I would be picked up.

The day of the wedding I did just that. I was driven to the house in a brand new shuttle bus. We arrived at a large beautiful brick mansion, very impressive. There are two circus size tents on the front lawn. Diane, the event coordinator is at the door giving instructions. She is all business. She says that the tents are for dinner and the ceremony will be out back. I ask how many guests are expected. She tells me 700. I asked her if she knew the budget for this event. She said that it was in the half million range.

"Out back" as she put it, are multi-leveled stone and brick patios opening out to a field as far as the eye can see. There are 7 or 8 large appetizer setups, first class food and elegance all the way. Crab legs, shrimp and lobster. A small orchestra, a jazz band, a rock band and a jester for the kids.

The bridal party all waited in the pool house. I had time to speak to fathers, moms, sisters, brothers, groomsmen and bridesmaids. The home belongs to the groom's parents, lovely people. Dad is a Wall Street hedge fund manager. Mom is a walking Redbook magazine cover. With the bride's father it gets interesting. I spoke to him extensively because it was wild talk. We talked about his many professions, gun runner for the Sandinistas, Alaskan fisherman, bush pilot, and "I can't tell you anything about what I did in the 1980's." Me: "Why not?" Him: "I just can't, man, I just can't."

So I did the ceremony, playing to a sea of 700 people.

I said my goodbyes to all and wished them well. Diane, the event coordinator, walked me to the front door. We exchanged pleasantries. She handed me an envelope and we said goodbye. On the shuttle back to my car I opened the envelope, $500 cash. I had eaten at least that much in crab and lobster.

The operatic wedding

A woman in her 40's called me and booked a wedding ceremony to be held at her New Canaan home. She was an opera singer, working in New York and London. She wanted a ceremony only, no rehearsal. She was going to have friends over the day before and they all would just talk about it. She lives on a beautifully landscaped mini estate. The house is a very picturesque New England Cape Cod. There is also a large converted barn which is her studio. She had many different ideas that she wanted to incorporate into the ceremony. I sent her five complete ceremonies as a jumping off point. We can build on what she chooses. After going around and around about the need for a rehearsal, I told her that I would come to her little rehearsal get together the day before. I wanted to make sure that she got what she wanted and was happy.

Many moons go by and the day of the wedding is fast approaching. In my tenth e-mail I tell her that it is down to the wire and I need the vows. She e-mails them two days later in garbled form. A scan of paper with nearly illegible writing and a lot of crossing out. It has no beginning and no ending. It certainly doesn't resemble a ceremony. A note written on the side says that this is what she wants to do, not necessarily in any order. She wants her large gay friend to be singing as she walks down the steps. They say an opera usually ends when the fat lady sings. The guy turns out to be hugely huge, flaming gay, and over the top funny. After that she wants him to read a few words that he has written about her and her fiancé. Then he is going to sing another song and then read a poem. She also wants him to participate in the Rose Ceremony portion of the ceremony, which usually involves only two. She has four friends that are going to read Shakespeare sonnets. Then his parents are going to read from Corinthians. They have three children that they want to be involved as well. The kids just wander around as we read.

From the angle of a planned ceremony, it was a complete disaster. However, nobody noticed, and it was a happy, fun event. Many hits and misses. I flirted with Tillie, a sharp, intelligent, attractive 80-year-old woman. We had a great conversation about New York in the 1940's and 50's.

On my way out I picked up a milkshake from a table as the fat man sang.

The Renaissance

I was asked if I would do a Renaissance Faire style wedding. It sounded cool so I accepted. The woman wanted me to wear a long brown monk's robe and asked if I had one. I told her that I didn't, but I would see what I could do. When I told my wife she said that she could easily make one, and she did. It was brown, of course, with a hood and had a gold rope belt. I wore sandals and I felt heavenly.

The ceremony was about one hour and twenty minutes north on Hammonasset Beach. I arrived there in street clothes. I wasn't going to drive around like a monk. Everyone was late. I wondered if I had the correct date. When I saw a jester and a princess arrive in a jeep, I was relieved. I changed into Mighty Monk. Within minutes 30 people showed up and most were dressed for the occasion. Commoners, maids, maidens, and knights. The beach was not crowded at all, but we did attract spectators. Some took pictures. The maiden of honor and a few commoners drew a big circle and placed lit candles all around.

I had met the bride and groom at my home a few months prior, but I did not see them this day until the ceremony began. The bride wore a simple white linen dress with a ring of flowers in her hair. The groom was in full medieval regalia. He had a black beard and wore a black outfit, knee high black boots and full chain armor and a helmet. He also had a huge shiny sword at his side. He was A Connecticut Yankee in King Arthur's Court.

The Black Knight and his fair maiden came forward and met in the circle in front of me. They had picked out old English wedding vows. At a given point the maid of honor handed me a rope which I used to tie the couple's wrists together, symbolizing being bound together for all eternity.

After we finished the ceremony and pictures were being taken and abundant kisses were exchanged, a woman came walking up the beach with a horse. This was unplanned. I suggested that the Black Knight borrow yon steed for a picture. Graciously the horse owner let everyone take pictures. We snapped a few of the bride on the horse, the groom standing next to her with the mighty monk holding the reins.

I asked the mother of the bride to send me the picture and she did. I've been looking for it ever since.

The runaway bride

I always call the happy couple a week or so ahead of each ceremony just to let them know I'll be there. Many people book a year in advance, so a call from the JP reassures them.

I remember the call I made a week before one couple's scheduled wedding.

I rang the guy and told him to expect me at the appointed date and time. He said, "Didn't Alexa call you? She said that she would call you." He began to apologize profusely. "I'm sorry man," he said. "But I am not getting married." I simply say, "Well, OK." and he tells me that she ran off with her old boyfriend two weeks ago. "She left town completely, gone. I hope this doesn't hang you up." I told him not to worry about me. He continued, and it sounded like a question, "I guess this means I'm really not getting married."

No need to apologize to me. I will forget about it in a week. This poor soul will remember this all his life!

The same shoes

A woman called and asked if I perform same-sex ceremonies in my home. I said that I did. She asked how much, and I gave her my lowest fee. She asked if I could do it tomorrow and could I do it for less. I got the vibe that she didn't have much to spend. My answers were yes and yes.

The next day they arrived. I met them at the door and escorted them in. They were a female couple in their 40's. The woman I had talked to was tall, attractive and wore a flowered dress. Her partner was short with a shaved head and wore a complete baseball uniform, red and white, #9. She also wore very cool red and white sneakers. It occurred to me that they were the same style my son had bought just the day before.

I read some vows that I borrowed from a Rainbow site. It only took a few minutes to make them happy. They were a gracious couple. They thanked me and headed out.

As they were walking to their car I ran upstairs and pulled my son to the window. "Look at her shoes," I said. In certain cases it's OK for a 13-year old to swear and this was one of them. He said, "Aw shit, Dad, I can never wear mine again."

The storm

I did a wedding on our historic Town Green. The Green has a gazebo set in a park. I have done many ceremonies there. It is only a 5-minute walk from my house.

On the day of these nuptials it was overcast with impending rain showers. I told the couple if it started to rain, we could go back to my house. When I got to the Green it was starting to sprinkle. By the time I got out of my car it had started to rain. As I ran to the gazebo it started to pour buckets. New England does this. It can be clear and sunny and within minutes it is a totally black sky. I am sure that within minutes it will be clear and sunny again. I got up the steps and into the gazebo just as a full-blown monsoon erupted. All this within about 3 minutes. The couple were already there with a few friends. The wind was fierce and cold. The rain was coming in sideways. I asked if they wanted to go to my house and the groom yelled above the howling wind, "No, let's just do it!" I almost had to scream to be heard over the thunder and lighting. It was wild and dangerous fun.

The tough guy

I saw this tough guy as soon as I entered the backyard. Elvis hair, Elvis sideburns, pencil thin mustache, black leather jacket, red shirt, black jeans and pointed black shoes. He was greeting each group of guests with, "What's up? Have a good time here." I wondered what his connection was to the couple getting married. For a second I thought that he may be hired entertainment. He looked like the Big Bad Wolf in a 1930's cartoon.

I found the couple in the house. Eventually I ask about the guy out in the yard. The groom says, "Sal? what a guy." Looking away, the bride says in a low muffled sarcastic tone, "Yeah, what a guy." The groom says that Sal is his mom's boyfriend. Right away I ask where mom might be. The bride says," In the shed." Jokingly I add, "tied up." Under her breath and without looking up the bride says, "I wish." The groom looks at her and tells her to cool it. I tell them that I will be outside when they are ready. What I really want to do is to engage with Sal/Elvis.

I introduce myself to Sal. I find that he is from Jersey, and that he makes wine, which is what has taken mom into the shed. At first he is friendly. Then he turns into a jerk. He insults ministers, judges, the law and marriage. In the middle of the tirade he says, "You want a drink, Padre?" I say no and that I am not a Padre. "What do I call you?" he asks. I tell him a simple "Sire" will do. "That's a title?" he asks. I say, "It is for you today." He gets it. He moves on, pointing back at me.

I was offered homemade wine out of the drain spout of a cooler. No thanks. I finished the ceremony and I left.

They took advantage of the situation

What I thought was going to be a small intimate gathering at my home turned out to be quite different indeed.

I didn't meet the couple until the evening of the ceremony. In the usual pre ceremony phone conversation they had asked if they could have a few guests. I said sure and asked how many? They said there would be about seven people including them. My living room can handle more than that.

I do many small ceremonies in my living room. The room is very large. The color is not red, but Crimson Lips. There are two large oak pocket doors that can be closed for privacy. The room has a few large palms and other foliage. At one end there is a 102-year-old built-in floor to ceiling Tiger Oak cabinet with leaded glass doors. A piano is on the other side. A few couches, a few chairs. I do the ceremonies in an alcove which has a beautiful tulip stained glass window set high on the wall. It is much warmer than City Hall and cheaper than renting a hall.

People arrived in two stretch limos, followed by five cars of guests. Everyone comes in and I am overwhelmed to say the least. There must be 35 people. In a matter of two minutes I went from alone and looking out the window and the next minute, instant party with a crowd I don't know. The bride and groom are in full wedding gear. White wedding dress and veil for her, a tux for the lucky man.

The groom says that they are waiting for Aunt Anne. I ask where Aunt Anne is coming from and he tells me, New Jersey. I excuse myself and go upstairs to hang out for as long as possible. Aunt Anne arrives. I have everyone gather around. We started and in five minutes it was over. They milled around, staying way too long.. Finally, they head for the door.

When I get to the porch behind all these bodies, I see on the walkway leading to the sidewalk 5 guys on either side holding up swords for the couple to walk through.

I notice a woman from my kid's school drive by looking a little perplexed. The guests are blowing bubbles and throwing rice. Without saying anything to me they all file into their respective cars and drive away.

This guy is a good catch

I married a couple who live right around the corner from me. Their home has lots of floor to ceiling windows. The river runs next to their property making for a beautiful view. They wanted a small simple ceremony, just them.

I think that it was raining so we decided on doing the ceremony in the living room. We stood in the middle of the room and I began. I asked if they had rings. The pretty bride said no, they did not. She adds that they are working on that.

I am reciting the vows and I say, "May I have the ring please?" The bride looks at me, cocks her head and adds a look of bewilderment. With that the groom pulls out a box. He opens and displays the ring which she immediately recognizes. She begins to weep softly and then she begins to cry. The man started to cry as well. I misted up myself.

This ring had been in the family for nearly 200 years. Unbeknownst to her, something the groom told me a few days prior, this wonderful man contacted the woman's grandmother in Germany and the grandmother sent him *her* grandmother's wedding ring.

This guy is a *great* catch.

What happens at the beach

I had this couple that wanted to get married on the beach at 7:30 am in New Haven, about 45 minutes from my house. I said yes. It was early, but OK. I can be back home by 9:30. They wanted to get married where and when they first met. No guests, just them.

I didn't see these people until the wedding. Our only contact is by phone. The guy has a very, very low gruff voice. He calls me every two or three days about stuff. With his last call he wants to change the time to 6:00 am as the sun is still coming up. I now must leave my house by 5:20 am, I am not liking this at all and his voice scares me.

I pull into the parking lot at the beach. I see two people that looked like they could be getting married. But it's not them. This area has a walkway on the sand. Houses line the beach facing it. The water is a long stretch across the sand. I walk to the top of a hill. Once there I see four people out on the point another half mile away. The sun is up, and dawn has turned into daylight. So much for getting up early and getting married at first light. I hike the rest of the way to the point in my suit, over sand, rocks, shells. The bride is wearing a beautiful wedding gown and the groom is in a tux. A photographer is taking pictures. They are standing in a marsh. The bottom of her wedding dress is wet and dirty. I wave hi and I sit on a bench next to a woman who is doing the bride's hair and makeup. The photographer knows that I am here. I wait patiently, but after about 15 minutes I had waited long enough. I stand and say, "Who wants to get married?" The bride says, "I do!" I stood on a rock and married them in the soggy marsh. Deed done. The groom forgot the marriage license in the car, so he ran off to get it. I said goodbye to the bride and the others and began to walk to meet the groom on his way back. I met up with him halfway and got the license. We hug and say goodbye.

As I was walking back near the top of the hill, two women in their 70's were standing talking. One asked if I had just married the couple out on the point. I answered yes. She then says, pointing to a bushy area, "Someone needs you over there." I just smile and keep walking. Then I see what she was talking about. On the sand between the bushes, two people were going at it hard and fast. Right in broad daylight on the beach in front of the fish and everyone. She was really vocal and had her legs wrapped tight around him.

As I walked to my car I looked back and I saw her sitting up, fixing her sweater. She stood up, brushed off some sand and slipped on her red underwear. He was laying on his side, already asleep.

Two Fall ceremonies

Today I did two weddings. Both were in beautiful New England autumn settings.

The first one was in an old historic tavern about 10 miles from my home. I booked this a year ago, so I didn't remember what the couple looked like and didn't remember them when I finally encountered them. The ceremony was taking place on the grounds of the tavern. There were pumpkins, mums, and a few Horns o' Plenty. The leaves on the trees were just turning yellow, gold and red. It was like being in a painting. We had handfasting.* The dad played the bagpipes. The maid of honor was exceptionally pretty. In this setting she looked like Alice in Wonderland. The bride did not smile once. I talked to her before, during and after the ceremony. Not once did that woman crack a smile. The groom was a pleasant enough guy. Good luck to that dude.

The second wedding on this same autumn day was on the beach in Westport. This girl must have e-mailed me 10 times about all kinds of things that only required a one- or two-word answer. She could have figured it out on her own.

*Handfasting is a Wikkan or Pagan custom, where hands are bound together in a ceremony.

This girl told me that I had married a friend of hers not long ago and that friend had recommended me. When I showed up at the rehearsal, I thought that I picked out the bride and said to her "Hi, Lauren." She said, "No, I am Fiona. You married me and my husband two years ago."

The bride and groom insisted that afterward I come for drinks at the marina just across the parking lot. I really don't drink, especially with people I don't know. Everyone drove. I was last. They all turned left to the club. I toiled over this so very hard as I came to the turn. I bowed out, turned right and sped away into the night.

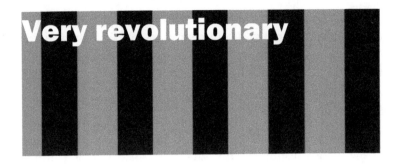

Very revolutionary

I did a ceremony at the historic Fairfield Burr Homestead in Fairfield, CT, which is about 10 miles up the Post Road. I remember the house. I had done two or three ceremonies there in the past.

Originally built in 1732, Thaddeus Burr, an uncle of Aaron Burr, and his wife Eunice lived in the home during the American Revolution. A dangerous time to live in Connecticut. In 1775 John Hancock married Dorothy Quincy at the Burr Homestead while Boston's patriotic activists fled the British. The home has also hosted George Washington, John Adams, and Samuel Adams. In 1779, it was set ablaze by the British and destroyed. Hancock insisted that the Burrs rebuild their home, which they did, completing it 11 years later.

The day of the wedding I was standing in the back garden as a van pulled up. The door opened and out came five or six actors with muskets, long rifles and dressed in 1776 period clothing. A Volkswagen pulled up a minute later carrying five women in the same era's vintage attire. The biggest one looked around and yelled, "Where's the rum?" The women began dancing around. A joyful bunch. They were here to provide a bit of whimsy, history, and merriment to today's reception.

The former Governor and other Connecticut notables were among the invitees. The bridal party was huge, 12 bridesmaids and an equal number of groomsmen. It came off perfectly, even though the bridal party was a small army. With the revolutionary actors in full character a good time was had by all!

I used a picture from that day for my website.

Wandering in the woods

A couple asked me to meet them at a nature preserve upstate to perform their ceremony in the woods. I asked if it was to be a formal affair and the groom said that it was. Even though it was only them and me. The wedding day was a hot one in July and it was a long ride. The air conditioner in my car needed freon and was not working well. That's how the day started.

I arrive at the entrance to the nature preserve and it is packed with cars, people and dogs. Many of the doggies were making fashion statements with scarves around their necks. Those dog owners are usually stoners. Dogs were running around everywhere acting nutty and carefree. I suspected that some of these dogs were high.

I had described my car to Rob, the groom. I was leaning on my car and from behind me I heard, "Dan?" I turned and saw a couple of Lederhosens standing there. It took a few seconds for my brain to compute this image. Not at all what I had expected to see. Lederhosen is the traditional German dress for Oktoberfest, like Heidi in the Alps. It turned out that he was German. The groom also had ported about 485 pounds of camera equipment with him. It looked heavy. The bride and I did wind up toting some of it. It was 90 + degrees, it was crowded, I was carrying my book of vows and his lenses box with a little broken handle. It was awkward. The trail was narrow, so it was difficult with passersby, AND I was in a black suit! It's a great thing to go hiking in dress shoes.

Rob could not find the right spot for the ceremony and the right setting for the wedding photos. We stopped a few times before he finally settled on a bend in the river. Hikers went by every few minutes. One wiseass hiker said, "Nice suit," as he walked by me.

So we do the ceremony and dozens of folks stop by to watch, yell, clap and hoot at the end. Then the picture taking begins. Rob asked if I could help out for a few minutes more with the cases. After about 20 minutes of this I finally had to excuse myself. I wished them well and I left. As I was walking out, I knew that it must be somewhat unusual to see a man deep in the woods wearing a suit.

Some teens in backward baseball hats were sitting on a table. As I walked by a girl said, "Why are you hiking in a suit?" Without looking at her, and not breaking my stride I said, "I woke up here, what day is it?" I continue down the path and I hear a kid say, "It's Tuesday."

Punk, it was Saturday.

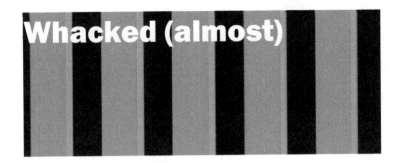

Whacked (almost)

I am sitting here on a snowy November night listening to "The End" by the Doors, thinking about a wedding I just performed today. I was afraid that the bride's father was going to kill me. That is a very strange feeling.

The bride, Dina, was about 22 years old, cute, short, very nervous and not too bright. The night before the ceremony at the rehearsal I found out that the wedding was changed from 6:00 p.m. to 5:00 p.m. This had been done a month prior and I didn't get the call. I had another ceremony booked for 4:30 p.m. The other wedding was scheduled to be a quick one at a private home in the same town. If they had held to the original hour I would have had plenty of time with some to spare. I figure that I could still make it, but it will be barely.

The next day I pulled into the parking lot for Dina's ceremony at exactly 5:00. The wedding is being held at an ethnic club. These clubs are quite numerous here in the northeast. This is where all the retired plumbers and contractors gather every day. They talk about the time Joey didn't beat that guy from the other neighborhood with a shovel and didn't bury him out in Jersey near Giants Stadium. They talk about the Mets or the Yankees, their wives and the old days because they are just regular guys. This place is kind of worn. A place where local meetings are held.

Standing on the deck is the bride's father. The guy is about 40 years old, 6' 4" and a lot more. He is wearing a black tux and looks like he is about to burst out of it. He reminds me of the Incredible Hulk, but not green. His head is shaved. He has tattoos swirling around his neck and has one too many piercings. He looked at me mean and hard and said, "You're late." Trying to avoid eye contact I glance to my left and I see a greasy guy probably named Vito, leaning on a car with New York plates. He is cleaning his fingernails with a knife and is wearing all black. I look back at the Hulk and he says, "I'm Dina's father." No way am I going to tell this gentleman that his daughter didn't call me about the time change. I say that I am sorry, but another ceremony went a little long. I put my hand out to shake and he turns and walks to the door. "This is the ceremony, pal," he snaps.

Soon I find myself in position, groomsmen and bridesmaids in place. The couple walks up the aisle and stands before me. Dina is short and her dress is very low cut This is a ridiculous wedding dress, way too revealing. My eyes travel from her bodice up right into her father's eyes. His killer look is aimed directly at me. He is standing about six feet away and he sees where I am looking. It still scares me as I write this..

After the ceremony, everyone went out on the deck and into the parking lot to take pictures. I said goodbye to the couple and headed out the door. I scanned for possible danger. I skirted the crowd and made it to my car. I pulled out of the lot with a "Whew." I'm aiming for the traffic light about 100 feet down the street and hoping that Vito doesn't pull up next to me, and I'm hoping that he doesn't look at me, and I hope he doesn't raise his arm and I hope he doesn't point a gun at me and I'm hoping he doesn't get a shot off before I can get away..

Me dying is not how I want my wise guy movie to end.

SECOND GUESS PRESS

Enjoy these titles published 2011-2020

111 Haiku by SMoss

24 Poems by Marco Fazzini

Air by Cat Soubbotnik

Anorexia Mon Amour by M.A.T

Blindés by Alexandre d'Huy

The Blue Tibetan Poppy by Margaret Sheffield

The Book of Deals by SMoss

Canto dell'isola by Marco Fazzini

Case Studies of Five Modern Labyrinths by SMoss

The Captain Blackpool Trilogy **The Crimson Garter** by SMoss

The Captain Blackpool Trilogy **Fate & the Pearls** by SMoss

Classic: A Love Letter to Milo Reice by Paula Sweet

Degenerate Work by Mike Berg

DO NOT – a book of rules by Paula Sweet

A Friendly Guide to the Marrakech Medina by Paula Sweet

The Grandpa Trio **Grandpa Goes Shopping** by Paula Sweet

The Grandpa Trio **Grandpa Does Yoga** by Paula Sweet

The Grandpa Trio **Grandpa Takes A Walk** by Paula Sweet

The History & Adventures of the Bandit Joaquin Murietta by SMoss

HACK IS BACK by SMoss

Hammam Ladies by Paula Sweet

Hitman in Delhi, a screenplay by Sean Rooney with SMoss

La Toux by Pierre d'Huy

Layers of Humankind/ Book 1: The Vision by Karl Stober

Leaving Your Dragon by SMoss

Legacy & Power by SMoss with Pierre d'Huy

Un livre des aquarelles by SMoss

Mandalas by Cat Soubbotnik

all available on Amazon

or visit www.secondguesspress.com